The Complete Guide to Tibetan Mastiffs

Tarah Schwartz

Foreword by Richard Eichhorn
Drakyi Tibetan Mastiffs

LP Media Inc. Publishing

Text copyright © 2020 by LP Media Inc.

www.lpmedia.org

Publication Data

Tarah Schwartz

The Complete Guide to Tibetan Mastiffs ---- First edition.

Summary: "Successfully raising a Tibetan Mastiffs from puppy to old age" --- Provided by publisher.

ISBN: 978-1-952069-05-5

[1.Tibetan Mastiffs --- Non-Fiction] I. Title.

Design by Sorin Rădulescu

First paperback edition, 2020

Cover Photo - Drakyi Leonidas, LEO
Photo Courtesy of Richard Eichhorn - Drakyi Tibetan Mastiffs

TABLE OF CONTENTS

FOREWORD

When this book was first introduced to me as a rough draft to review, I thought, "Who is this person, and what do they have to do with Tibetan Mastiffs?" With so much attention focused on the breed in recent years, a new, quality, authoritative breed publication would always be welcomed, but was this going to be the case? In the absence of my own cumulative, someday exposé on the breed, how would this book be received?

Photo Courtesy of Eric Schwabel

Richard Eichhorn with Drakyi Dawa Dominus

As I skimmed the chapters and then reviewed them in more depth, it became clear to me that author Tarah Schwartz had done her research and brought her know-how. She has years of advice from practical experience combined with a deep knowledge of canine welfare that will be of benefit to any dog owner. This is a book I can heartily recommend for the library of every Tibetan Mastiff enthusiast.

In the 1980s, I coauthored "The Tibetan Mastiff Owner's Manual" with my partner and breed mentor Linda Larsen, a booklet that we sent out with each puppy as it went to its new home. It offered tips on socialization, training, veterinary care, and nutrition. Fast-forward to 2020, and this book is an updated, comprehensive, expanded version and more, complete with breed-specific practical tips from Tibetan Mastiff owners and breeders, enhanced with beautiful breed photographs. And while there are any number of canine care books on the market, this book is a guide with tips specifically for the Tibetan Mastiff owner, with recommendations and answers to questions by owners on how to best care for dogs from puppy-hood through the late senior years.

My thanks go out to David Anderson and the publishing team for giving me the chance to review, contribute to, and edit The Complete Guide to Tibetan Mastiffs. I am happy for the association and to be able to endorse the author's efforts. Much appreciation to others in the Tibetan Mastiff community for their unique contributions and to those who have kindly shared the photographs used in this book. It has been an honor and privilege to be asked to write this foreword and to be able to welcome and recommend this detailed publication to Tibetan Mastiff lovers around the world.

Richard W. Eichhorn
Drakyi Tibetan Mastiffs
AKC Judge and Breed Specialist
www.tibetanmastiff.com

CHAPTER 1

The History of the Tibetan Mastiff

"A rare breed attracts rare people. In this case, intelligent, loyal, stubborn, independent people with strong-willed personalities."

Crystal Cosgrove
Adynasty Tibetan Mastiffs

Photo Courtesy
of Efrain Valle

3 month old LUNGJUNG, wearing the traditional Tibetan Kekhor collar

The Origins of the Tibetan Mastiff

The Tibetan Mastiff is a noble and imposing dog that is native to the Himalayan Mountains. It's estimated that the Tibetan Mastiff is old enough to be the original Mastiff, but unfortunately, accurate historical records do not exist. For much of Tibet's history, the country remained relatively isolated and few westerners were allowed access. From a historical perspective, it's not entirely accurate to describe the Tibetan Mastiff as a breed, but rather as a landrace. This is due to the fact that they have not always been bred with the preservation of a single breed in mind, but rather the breed was created from the interbreeding of dogs within a relatively isolated geographic region.

Traveler and writer Meer Izzut-Oollah encountered Tibetan Mastiff-type dogs in the early 1800s. According to Izzut-Oollah's book Travels in Central Asia in the Years 1812-13, "The dogs of Tibet are twice the size of those seen in India, with large heads and hairy bodies. They are powerful animals and are said to be able to kill a tiger. During the day they are kept chained up and are let loose at night to guard their masters' house."

As Izzut-Oolah claimed in his description of the breed, the Tibetan Mastiff was originally developed as a guardian. Traditionally, they were kept chained to discourage thieves and those with ill intent from entering homes. In nomadic communities and rural villages, the dogs were generally allowed to roam loose at night to protect community members and livestock from predators such as leopards, wolves, tigers, and bears.

Prior to the 19th and 20th centuries, few Tibetan Mastiffs left their Himalayan homeland. Those that were exported were likely given as gifts to explorers and dignitaries. Many believe that these early Tibetan Mastiffs were used as basic stock to create other Mastiff and working breeds. However, while other breeds were being developed using the exported Tibetan dogs, the Tibetan Mastiff itself remained relatively unchanged due to the isolation of the communities that bred them.

Thousands of years of development as a livestock and village guardian has resulted in a breed that is as fearless as it is loyal. Tibetan Mastiffs are patient protectors that are able to work independently to ensure the safety of their flock. Although there are few nomadic cultures left, the breed is still used today by Tibetans to protect their homes and property.

The Influence of the Tibetan Wolf

The harsh conditions of the Tibetan Plateau have required the Tibetan Mastiff to adapt to life at high altitudes. While some adaptations are rather obvious, such as the Tibetan Mastiff's insulating coat, others are a bit more subtle. At high altitude, lower air pressure makes it more difficult for oxygen to enter the bloodstream. This causes hypoxia, or oxygen deprivation, sometimes referred to as altitude sickness. Hypoxia is common among humans who take part in hiking or mountaineering at high altitude, but it can also affect animals who are unused to living at higher elevation. Most domestic dog breeds are unable to handle the effects of hypoxia, but the Tibetan Mastiff is an exception. Genetic researchers have discovered that Tibetan Mastiffs, unlike other domestic breeds, possess certain genes that allow them to avoid the detrimental effects of hypoxia. One gene in particular, known as EPAS1, is responsible for the production of hemoglobin in the bloodstream.

In a study headed by Zhen Wang and Yixue Li of the Shanghai Institutes for Biological Sciences (SIBS), the genomes of the Tibetan Mastiff were examined and compared to those of the Tibetan wolf, which is a subspecies of the gray wolf. In particular, researchers were interested in the genes re-

Photo Courtesy
of Maria Folkomina

*Photo Courtesy
of Tina De Boltz*

sponsible for the animals' ability to live at high altitudes, specifically two genes known as EPAS1 and HBB, which are common in wild animals living at high altitude. Scientists were interested in whether the Tibetan Mastiff's hypoxia-adaptive genes were a natural adaptation or had been inherited from their wild wolf ancestors.

Through extensive DNA research, scientists working at SIBS were able to determine that due to early interbreeding between Tibetan Mastiffs and Tibetan wolves, modern Tibetan Mastiffs displayed changes in certain genes. These changes have resulted in higher levels of hemoglobin in their blood than other domestic breeds native to lower altitudes have. The increased hemoglobin allows the breed to function better in low oxygen environments while avoiding hypoxia. This adaptation explains why the Tibetan Mastiff has been able to thrive at elevations around 15,000 feet or higher. Dogs brought into Tibet by travelers and nomads were less likely to survive the hypoxic conditions, so the native population was allowed to thrive unaltered by outside influence.

The Tibetan Mastiff in the Show Ring

Photo Courtesy of Carol Czerw

Ridgeland's Princess Amala

The first notable appearance of the Tibetan Mastiff outside its homeland was in 1847 when Lord Hardinge, Viceroy of India, sent a large dog from Tibet to Queen Victoria as a gift. England had just recently held its first dog show in 1859 and the popularity of purebred dogs was on the rise. In 1873, the Kennel Club was formed, officially creating the first Stud Book, which contained the pedigrees of 4027 individual dogs. The dog given to Queen Victoria, named Siring, was officially recorded as a Tibetan Mastiff.

Queen Victoria's Tibetan Mastiff Siring

Shortly after the Kennel Club's formation, two more Tibetan Mastiffs were brought to England by the Prince of Wales and shown at the Alexandra Palace Show in December 1875. From that point forward, there were only a few more imports of the breed to England and Europe. However, in 1928 the Honorable Colonel Bailey and his wife, Irma, imported four Tibetan Mastiffs that they had obtained while Colonel Bailey was stationed in Tibet. The couple were so taken with the breed that Mrs. Bailey formed the Tibetan Breeds Association in 1931. The Tibetan Breeds Association was the first to develop a breed standard for the Tibetan Mastiff. This standard would go on to be the first official standard for the breed recognized by the Kennel Club of England. The Federation Cynologique Internationale (FCI), which is the worldwide organization for dog sports, would also go on to recognize this breed standard.

Between World War II and the 1970s, very few, if any, Tibetan Mastiffs were imported into England. It wasn't until 1976 that imports resumed, and the breed began to grow in popularity. Due to the hard work and dedication of a few passionate breeders, the Tibetan Mastiff was recognized by the Kennel Club in 1998. Originally, the breed was categorized in the Miscel-

Photo Courtesy of R. Eichhorn, Michael & Linda Brantley

CH Drakyi Gold Standard, MIDAS. First AKC Best in Show winner in breed history

15

laneous Group before finally finding its home in the Guardian Dog Group alongside similar breeds.

On the other side of the Atlantic, little was known about the breed. In the late 1950s, President Eisenhower received two Tibetan Mastiffs as a gift from Tibet, but they were simply sent to live on a farm without further recognition. As in England, few dogs were imported into the US until the 1970s, when dedicated breeders began to seek out foundation stock. The breed did not gain traction as quickly as it did in England and Europe and was not fully recognized by the American Kennel Club until 2007, when the Tibetan Mastiff became the 155th breed recognized by the AKC and was officially placed in the Working Group.

The Tibetan Mastiff's Influence on Other Breeds

As one of the most ancient domestic dog landraces, the Tibetan Mastiff is often considered to be the foundation of many of today's Mastiff and guardian breeds. Ancestors of today's Tibetan Mastiff were used as both temple guardians and war party sentries. They accompanied armies of Assyrians, Persians, Huns, and Mongols as they traveled from battle to battle. Rather than being used as attack dogs, they were used to guard camps of warriors. This nomadic lifestyle led to Tibetan Mastiffs breeding with other types of dogs they encountered on their journeys.

Though little is known about the Tibetan Mastiff's past, many canine experts, known as cynologists, believe that the dogs of these nomadic cultures became the foundation for many of today's working and guardian breeds. Their innate sense of duty, fearlessness, and loyalty were prized characteristics that were passed on through generations. It's easy to see why those who encountered the breed were eager to cross the dogs with their own working, herding, or guardian dogs to create more specialized breeds while still maintaining the best qualities of the Tibetan Mastiff.

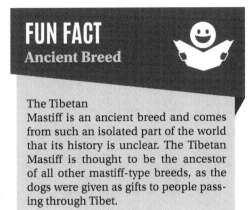

FUN FACT
Ancient Breed

The Tibetan Mastiff is an ancient breed and comes from such an isolated part of the world that its history is unclear. The Tibetan Mastiff is thought to be the ancestor of all other mastiff-type breeds, as the dogs were given as gifts to people passing through Tibet.

The Most Expensive Dog in the World

In March 2014, the Tibetan Mastiff breed made international headlines after a dog was sold at a luxury pet fair in China. The pet fair, held in the eastern province of Zhejiang, is a popular place for China's wealthy upper class to buy rare and exotic pets. After selling for a whopping 12 million yuan, or nearly $2 million, the young Tibetan Mastiff officially became the most expensive dog in the world. Measuring 31 inches tall and weighing nearly 200 pounds, the young male was an impressive example of his breed.

However, this is not the first time the Tibetan Mastiff has made headlines for selling at an incredibly high price. In 2011 an 11-month-old Tibetan Mastiff puppy named Big Splash was sold at a similar event for $1.5 million. At that time, Big Splash was the most expensive dog ever sold.

Although rare in many places around the world, including their native Tibet, Tibetan Mastiffs are becoming increasingly popular in China. The Associated Press has even referred to them as the "dog of the moment" in China due to their popularity among China's most wealthy citizens. Purebred dogs and Tibetan Mastiffs in particular, have become a status symbol, similar to expensive sports cars and luxury mansions. At one pet fair in Xi'an, a Tibetan Mastiff named Yangtze River 2 was purchased for approximately $600,000 and escorted to his new home in his owner's fleet of Rolls Royces. Due to their rarity, mysterious past, and impressive and foreboding appearance, it's no wonder Tibetan Mastiffs have become the most expensive breed in the world.

CHAPTER 2
The Tibetan Mastiff

Physical Characteristics

"Their beautiful mane and thick coats are breathtaking to behold, coupled with the unique profile of the tail carried over the back makes them quite unique. While they look huge in reality they are an agile and athletic dog, which makes them able to move quite quickly when they want to."

Michael Brantley
Dreamland Kennel

Photo Courtesy of Cristopher Shirk

Capper Mountain Flight of the Monarch

Tibetan Mastiffs are large dogs with a noble and impressive appearance. They are slightly longer than they are tall. At maturity, males typically measure 26 to 29 inches at the withers and weigh 90 to 150 pounds. Females are a bit smaller, measuring 24 to 27 inches tall at the withers and weighting 70 to 120 pounds. Tibetan Mastiffs are a slow growing breed, usually not reaching physical maturity until around 18 months of age. At 18 months, any males measuring under 25 inches and females under 23 inches are disqualified from the conformation ring. In competition, there is no preference given to larger dogs so long as they meet the rest of the requirements of the breed standard.

According to the contemporary standards, Tibetan Mastiffs have a strong, broad head with heavy brow ridges. Heavy wrinkling on the head will be severely faulted in the show ring, but a single fold around the face is acceptable. Facial expression is an essential characteristic of the breed. They should appear watchful, aloof, and intelligent. The eyes are expressive and are always brown in color. The rims of the eyes should always be black except in blue or gray dogs, in which case they should be the darkest shade of gray possible. The almond-shaped eyes are set well apart and are slightly slanted. The Tibetan Mastiff's muzzle should be broad and square when viewed from any side. The nose should be black, except in gray or blue dogs, when it should be dark gray. On brown dogs, the nose will be a dark shade. The teeth of the Tibetan Mastiff are large, strong, and should meet in a scissor bite. The ears are medium-sized, V-shaped, and should be level with the top of the skull. They drop forward and hang close to the head but are raised when alert. The hair on the ear should be short and soft.

The Tibetan Mastiff's neck should be well muscled and moderately arched, long enough to appear balanced with the body. A moderate dewlap, or fold of skin, is allowed. In adult dogs, the neck will be covered in a thick mane of hair. When viewed from the side, Tibetan Mastiffs should display a level topline. The chest is deep and well developed and there should be a pronounced tuck-up along the belly. The legs are straight, with substantial muscle and bone with a slight slope at the pasterns. The feet resemble cat feet in shape and may have feathering between the toes. Toenails may be either black or white, depending on the dog's coat color. Some Tibetan Mastiffs will have single dewclaws on the front legs and either single or double dewclaws on the hind legs. The tail of the Tibetan Mastiff is heavily feathered and set high on the back. When alert or while the dog is moving, the tail is carried curled over the back, but is usually carried down when the dog is relaxing.

Male Tibetan Mastiffs typically have a thicker coat than females, but in both genders the quality of the coat is considered to be more important than the length. This is a double-coated breed, with long, coarse guard hairs and a soft, heavy undercoat. The coat should never be curly, wavy, or silky in texture. Rather, the undercoat should feel woolly. The neck and shoulders are heavily coated, especially in males. The tail and britches are also heavily feathered. In the show ring, Tibetan Mastiffs are not to be trimmed, except to tidy the feet and hocks.

Tibetan Mastiffs come in a variety of colors. The American Kennel Club accepts Tibetan Mastiffs in black, brown, and blue or gray, all of which may or may not have tan markings on the face, feet, legs, and tail. Gold is also an accepted color, but it may range from a true golden color similar to that of a Golden Retriever to a deep reddish gold. Gold dogs may also display varying degrees of sable markings. Small white markings on the chest and feet are acceptable, but large white markings will be faulted in the show ring. Any other color will be disqualified.

Photo Courtesy of Marc & Laurel Denk

CH Lafahhs Lokapala Drakyi, LOKA

Behavioral Characteristics

Tibetan Mastiffs are naturally aloof dogs who tend to be wary of strangers. Without socialization, this can result in an aggressive dog who will fearlessly defend his family and property against any perceived threat. While this was a valued trait of the breed in the past, it can cause problems for inexperienced owners. Training and socialization must begin as early

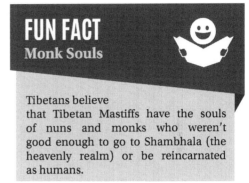

FUN FACT
Monk Souls

Tibetans believe that Tibetan Mastiffs have the souls of nuns and monks who weren't good enough to go to Shambhala (the heavenly realm) or be reincarnated as humans.

as possible to allow a dog to develop the confidence and knowledge needed to make the right decisions regarding who is and is not allowed in his home.

As temple and village guardians, Tibetan Mastiffs were bred to work independently and without regular direction from their human pack members. This has resulted in a breed that will often choose to make decisions on its own rather than listen to direction. This independent streak can be a challenge in training. If you're looking for a dog to compete in obedience or agility, you'll need to reconsider your choice of breed, as the Tibetan Mastiff is more likely to follow his own agenda than to listen to your every command.

The Tibetan Mastiff's unwillingness to listen to your commands should not be mistaken for stupidity. This breed is incredibly intelligent and perceptive. Remember, they were bred to think independently and are capable of making complex decisions based on their own knowledge and experiences. It's not that they are incapable of learning a variety of tricks and commands, it's just that they believe they have better things to do. It should be noted that Tibetan Mastiffs can become rather destructive if they are not given an outlet for their intelligence. This breed requires significant mental stimulation in order to deter destructive habits from developing. Dogs who are left to their own devices are likely to begin looking for ways to entertain themselves, which may include shredding pillows, chewing up furniture, and digging up your flower garden. However, with enough mental exercise, the Tibetan Mastiff can make a wonderful family companion or show dog. They do especially well with other canine companions to play with.

Potential Problems with Large Breeds

"TM's are barkers and chewers by nature, so learn to adapt to that and provide the environment and chew toys to avoid destruction of things you don't want."

Debbie Parsons Slayton
Dreamcatcher Tibetan Mastiffs

When bringing home a large breed, such as the Tibetan Mastiff, it's important that you establish the rules of your home right away. Without proper training and guidance, large dogs can quickly become unmanageable. Remember, Tibetan Mastiffs are strong and powerful, and it's unlikely that you'll be able to safely outmuscle them. This means teaching them to walk politely on a leash, greet people without jumping on them, and move off the furniture when asked. Although Tibetan Mastiffs can be a challenge to train, they can quickly detect whether or not you mean what you're asking of them. If they determine that you are unwilling to back up your demands, they are likely to ignore you completely. However, if you establish your po-

Photo Courtesy of
Richard Eichhorn & Efrain Valle
Drakyi Tibetan Mastiffs

Drakyi Leonidas, LEO

sition as leader of the pack and consistently enforce the rules of the house, your Tibetan Mastiff will quickly understand what is expected of him. Tibetan Mastiffs are incredibly intelligent dogs, so they will learn habits, both good and bad, in a short period of time.

Gastric Dilation Volvulus, also known as GDV or bloat, is a common condition in large breed dogs, though it can happen in smaller breeds as well. This medical emergency occurs when a dog's stomach fills with air. As the pressure builds, it can limit circulation and send the dog into shock. Without treatment, the condition can be fatal. However, there are steps that can be taken to prevent the most severe cases of bloat. These will be discussed more in detail in Chapter 8.

Tibetan Mastiffs as Family Dogs

Before welcoming a Tibetan Mastiff into your home as a family dog, you need to consider the possible challenges you may face. Supervision is necessary any time children and dogs are interacting. Tibetan Mastiffs are large dogs who are often unaware of their size and power. Although it's unlikely your new dog will mean to harm your children, an overly enthusiastic Tibetan Mastiff can easily knock down a small child or toddler. When raised together from the beginning, Tibetan Mastiffs can make great companions for children, but care must be taken to nurture a healthy relationship. According to Debbie Mayer of Noble Legacy Tibetan Mastiffs, "It is never advisable to leave a dog alone with a young child, not because the dog's temperament is unpredictable so much as the child's behavior is unpredictable." Before you even bring your new dog home, it's a good idea to explain to your children how to properly interact with a dog. Setting up rules for both kids and dogs can go a long way toward ensuring a safe and comfortable environment for everyone.

As an ancient guardian breed, Tibetan Mastiffs are naturally suspicious of strangers and proper socialization is essential. Without socialization, Tibetan Mastiffs may take their guardian instincts too far. They may strongly defend their family and home against any perceived threat. This fearless breed will take on a potential threat without any hesitation, so you need to make sure that your new dog understands when this type of behavior is appropriate. Exposing your Tibetan Mastiff to as many different types of people, pets, and situations as possible will help him to become a confident companion who knows when it's appropriate to protect his family. This is not to say that with enough socialization your Tibetan Mastiff will be as friendly as the neighbor's Golden Retriever. Tibetan Mastiffs tend to be aloof and more interested in their job than with making new friends. This is a trait that has been developed in the breed over thousands of years, and you can't simply train it out of them.

It bears repeating that Tibetan Mastiffs are also highly intelligent dogs with an independent attitude. As a result, they can be challenging to train. According to Richard Eichhorn of Drakyi Tibetan Mastiffs, "while these dogs are intelligent to a fault, they often choose not to listen or obey, seemingly fulfilling some higher calling." If you're looking for an obedient dog who will respond to each and every command you give him, the Tibetan Mastiff may not be the breed for you. They are not untrainable, but you must be willing to stay committed and consistent in your training. Tibetan Mastiffs will lose interest quickly, so short but frequent training sessions are usually best.

If you live in a heavily populated neighborhood, you may need to manage your Tibetan Mastiff's schedule in order to keep your neighbors hap-

Photo Courtesy
of Richard Eichhorn
Drakyi Tibetan Mastiffs

CH Timberline Barni Drakyi, BARNES at 7 years, the Premiere Westminster Best of Breed.

py. It's not uncommon for guardian breeds, like the Tibetan Mastiff, to bark during the night. It will be nearly impossible to train your dog out of this habit, as it will go against all his instincts, so you'll need to manage his schedule instead. If night barking will be a problem in your area, you might find it easier to simply keep your Tibetan Mastiff indoors, rather than allow him to roam your property at night keeping the neighbors awake.

Tibetan Mastiffs as Livestock Guardian Dogs

"They are guardians; their judgment of character is keen and has to be managed appropriately."

Debbie Parsons Slayton
Dreamcatcher Tibetan Mastiffs

Although the dogs were traditionally used as temple and village guardians, the American Tibetan Mastiff Association (ATMA) does not recommend using modern Tibetan Mastiffs as full-time guardians. This is because in order to fulfill the duties of full-time guardians, dogs must be left to work with little or infrequent human interaction. This can result in a dog that will aggressively guard his home or flock against intruders, including any humans living on or visiting the property. Put simply, the ATMA believes the risk of danger is too great when Tibetan Mastiffs are raised with limited human interaction. Even in their native Tibet, the dogs are not simply left to do their jobs. Instead, it's best to welcome the dog into your home as part of the family, only allowing him to guard part-time. In Tibet, dogs are often allowed to roam free at night to protect their property and families.

It's important to understand that even as livestock guardians, Tibetan Mastiffs must be kept in a fenced area for their own protection. As Richard Eichhorn of Drakyi Tibetan Mastiffs explains, "Their concept of their home turf goes beyond the fence line, and underground electric fencing with a shock collar is useless in this breed. Between their desire to explore their turf and their high pain tolerance, they would rather endure the voltage." Whether you're hiking in the mountains or simply walking around the neighborhood, you need to make sure that you always keep your Tibetan Mastiff on-leash. Keeping your Tibetan Mastiff on a leash or behind a fence will ensure that he stays safe and out of trouble.

Photo Courtesy of Nicole Moss

Inexperienced Owners Beware

Tibetan Mastiffs are not the ideal dog for every family. If you have little experience dealing with headstrong, independent breeds, you may want to reconsider bringing a Tibetan Mastiff into your home. There are plenty of other breeds that are better suited for inexperienced owners. If you do not have the time and patience to properly socialize and train your Tibetan Mastiff, there is every possibility that you are going to end up with an aggressive or unmanageable dog. You need to be able to dedicate enough time to working with your dog to set him up for success. This means welcoming the dog into the family rather than allowing him to guard your property with little human interaction.

When properly trained and socialized, Tibetan Mastiffs make wonderful dogs for show or companionship, but they require a lifelong commitment from their owners. If you start basic obedience training as soon as you bring your new dog home, you'll begin establishing the rules and expectations necessary for your dog to become a well-behaved and responsible member of the family. You also need to make sure that your home is properly set up for a Tibetan Mastiff. This is not a breed that will do well off-leash, so you need to be certain that your entire property is secure and that your dog cannot escape. If you have any doubts about whether you are prepared to make this commitment, you may want to consider breeds other than the Tibetan Mastiff.

CHAPTER 3
Where to Find Your Tibetan Mastiff

"While the Tibetan Mastiff is famed as a caretaker of its village, those of us involved with these dogs take pride in being caretakers of the breed, to preserve and protect their ability to work and always recognizing a spiritual connection to their people."

Carol Gordon
Kachar Village Tibetan Mastiffs

Photo Courtesy
of Carol Czerw

Adopting an Adult vs Puppy

Before you begin searching for your new Tibetan Mastiff, you'll need to have some idea of what you're looking for. First, you'll need to decide whether you'd prefer to bring home an adult or a puppy. Both puppies and adult dogs have pros and cons, but it's up to you to decide what's best for you and your family.

FUN FACT
Winter Puppies

Most female Tibetan Mastiffs, go into heat once a year, usually in the late fall. As a result, the majority of Tibetan Mastiff puppies are born between November and January

Bringing home an adult dog can have both benefits and challenges. Depending on where you adopt your adult Tibetan Mastiff from, as well as his or her individual circumstances, you may be bringing a fairly well-trained dog into your home. Adult dogs have already gone through their destructive and obnoxious puppy stages, including teething and housetraining. Many adult dogs already know the basic rules of living in a house, as well as basic obedience commands. However, it is possible that you will be inheriting behavioral problems that were developed in the dog's previous home. While many dogs end up in shelters or rescues due to no fault of their own, many are given up because of training or behavioral issues. If you choose to bring home an adult dog, you'll need to decide if there any behaviors that you would consider to be dealbreakers. For instance, if you have other pets in your home, a Tibetan Mastiff that's aggressive to other dogs would not be an option. However, if you're willing to dedicate enough time and energy to your dog's training, you may be able to overcome many problem behaviors.

If you plan on bringing home a puppy, you'll also be facing a unique set of challenges and opportunities. On one hand, you'll be starting with a blank slate in terms of training. You won't have any behavioral problems or bad habits from previous homes, and you'll be able to train the dog as you like. However, you'll also need to work through the more frustrating aspects of puppy ownership. As your puppy's adult teeth begin to come in, you may find him chewing on inappropriate items around the house, such as shoes and furniture. Although not all adults will be housetrained, you can be certain that this is something you'll need to teach your new puppy. If you're indifferent to dealing with these problems and are confident in your abilities as a dog trainer, you may be able to consider bringing home a dog of any age, but if you have a preference, it's important to consider it before you begin searching for your ideal Tibetan Mastiff.

Purchasing from a Breeder vs Adopting from a Shelter

The decision to bring home a Tibetan Mastiff can be both exciting and intimidating, but it's important to keep your long-term goals in mind when choosing a dog. First, you'll need to consider why you want to bring a Tibetan Mastiff into your home and what your expectations are. If you're looking for a show dog or potential breeding stock, you may find that a breeder will be better able to find your dream dog. However, if you're simply looking for a companion for your family, you may be able to find the perfect dog at a shelter or breed rescue. You'll also need to decide how much of a hurry you are in to bring a new dog home. Many breeders only have a few litters per year, and you may need to be on a waiting list for some time. Likewise, Tibetan Mastiffs are not a common breed and it may be a challenge to find one in any local shelters or rescue groups.

Reputable breeders are one of the best places to find your dream dog, regardless of whether you want an adult or a puppy. Although many people think that you can only get a puppy from a breeder, it's not uncommon for breeders to have retired show dogs or breeding stock looking for a new home. As long as you're purchasing a dog from a reputable

Photo Courtesy
of Jordan and Amanda Seevers

Photo Courtesy of Nicole Moss

breeder who seeks to improve the breed with each generation, you can be sure that you're getting a healthy, high-quality dog. Before you sign any contracts or commit to bringing a dog home, be sure to do your research to make sure that the breeder you're buying your Tibetan Mastiff from has a good reputation. Good breeders will ask you nearly as many questions as you ask them in order to determine whether you are the right home for their dog.

Adopting a Tibetan Mastiff from a shelter or rescue is a great opportunity to improve the life of a homeless dog. However, you will still need to do your research to make sure that the shelter you're adopting from has a reputation for taking good care of the animals in their possession. As Tibetan Mastiffs can be somewhat difficult to find outside of breeders, you may not be able to find one at your local animal shelter. You will likely be more successful if you look for breed rescues or organizations that specialize in large and giant breed dogs. The advantage of finding a dog through one of these organizations is that they will have a better understanding of the breed and their unique needs and will be able to work with you to find the perfect dog.

Rescuing a Tibetan Mastiff

If you plan on rescuing your new Tibetan Mastiff from either a breed rescue or shelter, you should be aware that you'll likely have to undergo a bit of scrutiny before they allow you to take a dog home. Applications are an integral part of pet adoption and you'll need to be completely honest about your home and lifestyle. Most adoption applications will ask you about your home, family, lifestyle, and ability to financially care for a new pet. Remember, rescue staff and volunteers are not judging you, they simply want to make sure that your life is ideal for a unique breed like the Tibetan Mastiff. It can be a stressful experience for a dog to be adopted into a home, only to be returned to the shelter after a few days or weeks, so rescue staff simply want to reduce the risk of the dog being passed around more than necessary. Adoption applications can take time, as many rescues are run by volunteers who have other commitments in addition to reading through applications. By the time a volunteer can read through your application, the dog you had your eye on may have already found a home. To avoid this disappointment, it's best to fill out an application with the organization before choosing a dog. This will also enable rescue staff to help guide your choice according their knowledge of the dogs within their system.

Many rescues also require potential adopters to undergo a home check, where a rescue volunteer or staff member visits your home to make sure it's a safe and ideal environment for a Tibetan Mastiff. They are looking at

Photo Courtesy of Richard Eichhorn & Efrain Valle Drakyi Tibetan Mastiffs

Six week old Drakyi puppies

things like how much space you have, whether your property is fenced, and whether your home is secure enough to prevent a new dog from escaping. It can be a little stressful to invite someone into your home like this, but understand that they only have the dog's best interest in mind and do not care about your décor. Unless the problems are significant, they are unlikely to deny your application on the spot and will instead give you the opportunity to fix them.

Questions to Ask Before Bringing a Tibetan Mastiff Home

When speaking with a breeder or rescue staff member regarding a potential adoption, it's important to make sure you're bringing home a healthy Tibetan Mastiff. You should ask about the dog's health history and whether he has had any health problems in the past. This is also a great time to discuss any health testing of the dog's parents with the breeder. It's vital that you also inquire about the dog's vaccination history, deworming, and whether the dog has been spayed or neutered.

The most important questions you ask should be about the Tibetan Mastiff's behavior. You want to make sure you're bringing the right dog into your home. Regardless of whether you've chosen an adult or puppy, you should ask about the dog's temperament and how he reacts to new situations. Be sure to ask specifically about his interactions with children and other animals, especially if you have both in your home. While Tibetan Mastiffs can be standoffish with strangers, you want to make sure you aren't adopting a dog that has shown aggression toward humans in the past.

If you've chosen to adopt your new Tibetan Mastiff from a shelter, it can also be helpful to ask the shelter staff how the dog ended up in the shelter. Most dogs end up in shelters through no fault of their own. Often, the previous family's lifestyle changed, or they moved and were unable to keep the dog. However, if the dog was given up for behavioral issues it's important to know what you're getting yourself into and whether you're prepared for the training commitment involved in solving those problems.

If you've chosen to purchase a Tibetan Mastiff from a breeder, you should also make sure that the dog will help you meet your long-term goals. If you're looking for a show dog, it's important to discuss this with the breeder to make sure you're taking the right dog. Not all puppies from a litter are destined for the show ring, so if you have specific goals in mind the breeder will be able to help you choose the right dog.

When you choose to adopt a puppy, you're doing so with the understanding that training will be your responsibility. However, owners who choose to adopt adults often do so with the expectation that the dog is past many of the annoying stages of puppyhood. If you're adopting an adult Tibetan Mastiff, you might consider asking about his or her level of training. Ask about whether the dog is housetrained, if he recognizes his name, and what commands he may know. While basic training is unlikely to be a dealbreaker, it's still helpful to know where you'll need to start with training when you get home.

Regardless of how or what you intend to feed your new Tibetan Mastiff, you should ask about his mealtime habits and what food he is currently eating. Knowing what type of food he is eating at the shelter or the breeder's home will allow you to either continue feeding what he's used to or slowly transition him onto the food of your choice. It's also helpful to know if he's a polite eater or if he gulps his food. Food aggression can be a difficult habit to break, so if your new dog has any behavioral problems with food, you'll need to be aware of this before you take him home.

Remember, each dog is an individual and has its own unique likes, dislikes, and needs. Moving into a new household can be stressful for a dog so it's worth asking the breeder or shelter staff if your new Tibetan Mastiff has any unique preferences. Maybe he likes a certain kind of toy, prefers to sleep with a blanket, or doesn't like eating out of a certain type of dish. By the time puppies are old enough to go to their new homes, they've all begun developing unique personalities and the breeder will be able to tell you any unique characteristics about the puppy you've chosen. Adult dogs have often had time to develop interesting habits or preferences in their previous homes so breeders and shelter staff members should be able to give you some idea on how to make this difficult transition easier on your new Tibetan Mastiff.

Choosing to bring a Tibetan Mastiff into your home is a big responsibility and will require a commitment from each and every family member. You're adopting the dog with the understanding that you're willing to provide him with a loving home for as long as possible. However, life often changes in ways we do not expect. Sometimes certain bad habits or problems may appear after spending time with your new dog. Even if you're willing to work through any problems, it's still worth asking the breeder or rescue staff about their return policy. If you take the dog home for several days, weeks, or even years and things don't work out, it's good to know that the dog has somewhere to go. Breeders often include a clause about circumstances like this in their contract, so don't be afraid to ask for more information.

Choosing a Reputable Breeder

"I recommend that anyone looking at owning a TM buy from a breeder who shows and does the requisite health testing. A breeder who shows their dogs has spent the time to socialize their breeding stock and selected them for not only their conformation but their temperament as well."

Michael Brantley
Dreamland Kennel

When you begin searching for a Tibetan Mastiff, it's essential that you don't just choose the first breeder you find on the internet. In order to en¬sure that you're getting a healthy, quality purebred dog, you need to be will¬ing to do a little research. If you do choose to find a breeder on the internet, there are a few qualities you can look for to distinguish a reputable breed¬er from a breeder who regards their income above the well-being of their dogs. The American Kennel Club offers a page on their website called the AKC Marketplace (https://marketplace.akc.org/) where you can search for puppies and breeders. The AKC allows breeders to list their most note-worthy achievements along with their litter advertisement. You can also search pedigree records to verify the ped¬igrees of individual dogs. The Orthopedic Foundation for Animals (OFA) also allows the general public to search their Canine Health Information Center (https://www.ofa.org/about/chic-program) for records and results of health testing.

One of the best ways to find a reputable breeder is to ask other Tibetan Mastiff owners where they acquired their dogs. Try going to local dog shows or competitions. This will also give you a chance to see what type of dogs these breeders are producing. If you meet a few dogs from the breeder that have personalities or appearances that don't appeal to you, you'll know that you need to keep searching. On the other hand, if you meet a dog that is everything you're looking for in a Tibetan Mastiff, talk with the owner and find out where the dog came from. Owners and handlers will also be able to answer any lingering questions you may have about the breed before you commit to finding a breeder.

A reputable breeder will always prioritize the well-being of their dogs over everything else. They seek to improve the quality and health of the breed as a whole with each generation. In order to accomplish this, they are extremely picky about which dogs are bred and which should not be allowed to reproduce.

Reputable breeders will also be happy to discuss their dogs' performance records. Some may even have this information published on their website. While performance records might not mean much to someone looking for a family companion, if you're looking for a future show ring star, this is crucial information. However, even for dogs destined for the family home, knowing that your new dog's pedigree is made up of the best the breed has to offer will give you peace of mind knowing that with the right training, your dog can become an ambassador for the breed, even if he doesn't end up in the winner's circle.

Most importantly, you need to find a breeder that's willing to work with you to find you the ideal dog. A good breeder will ask you as many questions as you ask them. In a way, they are interviewing you to make sure their dog will be going to the right home. If they feel that you are a good match for the breed, the breeder will work hard to find you the perfect puppy. Try to avoid any breeder that tries to talk you into buying a puppy without making sure you're a good match. Reputable breeders don't need to push their puppies onto potential owners. Rather, many top breeders have long waiting lists and people often line up to make sure they end up with the perfect dog.

Contracts and Guarantees

When purchasing a purebred puppy, it's almost guaranteed that the breeder will ask that you sign a contract. Contracts are meant to protect both you and the breeder financially while prioritizing the puppy's wellbeing. The contract will also specify which dog you're taking home, how much you paid, and the conditions of the purchase, as well as the breeder's guarantees.

On the owner's side, signing the contract means that you agree to take on the responsibility of the puppy's health and wellbeing. Breeder's contracts often include clauses about regular immunizations, health checks, and spaying or neutering at an appropriate age. Most breeders will require dogs adopted into pet homes to be spayed or neutered, whereas most show dogs will need to remain unaltered in order to compete. Some breeders will even return a portion of your original deposit once you provide proof that the puppy has been spayed or neutered.

Some breeders may also specify within their contract what type of food they want you to feed the puppy. Most breeders are lifelong dog owners and through trial and error have found what type of food works best for their dogs. After finding a diet that their dogs thrive on, they often prefer that their puppies continue to eat that way throughout their life-time. Breeders that are dedicated raw feeders will often only allow their puppies to go to families who intend to continue feeding their dog a raw diet.

Photo Courtesy of R. Eichhorn and E. Valle

BRAVO at 12 weeks

Contracts will also contain a section guaranteeing that the puppy you're buying is free from any genetic diseases or disorders common to the breed. As long as the breeder has properly health tested the parents, the risk of this is low, but it's still an essential part of the contract. If a puppy tests positive or is diagnosed with any of the conditions listed, the contract should also state what actions are to be taken by both the breeder and the owner. In many cases, owners will have already fallen in love with the puppy and will choose to keep it regardless of health, but some may also choose to return the puppy to the breeder. In the case of the puppy's death due a disease or illness originating from the breeder's care, the contract may guarantee either a refund or a replacement puppy from a litter in the future.

Nearly all breeders will also include a statement in their contracts regarding what to do if the owner is no longer able or willing to care for the puppy. Most breeders will readily take a dog back at any time and for any reason, whether it's due to behavioral problems or a change in lifestyle. This is done to prevent the dog from ending up in either a shelter or an inappropriate home. This section of the contract may also include what's referred to as a 'happiness clause'. If you are unhappy with your new Tibetan Mastiff, for any reason, you can return the dog to the breeder with no questions asked. The contract should also state whether a refund will be provided in this case.

It's crucial that you read the contract thoroughly before signing it or committing to the purchase of a Tibetan Mastiff. If you have any questions regarding the content of the contract, be sure to ask the breeder. Remember, the contract exists to protect both you and the breeder, as well as the puppy. It's also a legally binding document so you need to make sure you're aware of what you're agreeing to before you sign it.

Health Testing and Certifications

Reputable breeders will always test their Tibetan Mastiffs for common genetic disorders in order to improve the breed's health as a whole. If an individual dog does not pass one or more of the tests with a satisfactory rating, the breeder will likely spay or neuter the dog to prevent the problem from being passed on to future generation. This often applies to carriers of certain diseases, regardless of whether they exhibit any symptoms. Good breeders will always be dedicated to the wellbeing of the breed and health testing and certifications allow them to monitor the progress of their breeding program.

The Orthopedic Foundation for Animals (OFA) is one of the leading organizations in canine genetic research. They have a database containing the test results of thousands of individual dogs of nearly every breed. Breeders and owners alike can have their dogs tested by local veterinarians and submit the results to the OFA for assessment for a nominal fee. Each breed has a number of recommended tests based on common disorders known to afflict the breed. Most test results require the dog to be fully grown, usually over 12 or 18 months of age, but some cannot be performed until the dog is two years of age. Once the required and optional test results are submitted, the results are recorded within the OFA's Canine Health Information Center and individual dogs are given a CHIC number. These results are then made publicly available on the OFA's website and can be searched by using the dog's name or CHIC number. If the breeder you're working with does not provide you with these results, you can easily search for them on the OFA's website to verify what the breeder has told you.

For Tibetan Mastiffs, the OFA recommends testing for hip and elbow dysplasia, as well as autoimmune thyroiditis. Dogs must also undergo an eye examination by an ophthalmologist certified by the American College of Veterinary Ophthalmologists. Once individual dogs have undergone all of the required tests, their results are posted publicly to the OFA's website and can be searched for by name or registration number. A quality breeder will not be shy about sharing these results with potential adopters.

Adopting an Adult Dog

When you decide to bring home an adult Tibetan Mastiff, you need to realize that the transition isn't going to be smooth sailing. Even though you're bringing home an adult dog, he will still go through a stressful transition period. Perhaps your new dog has lived with the same family his whole life, or it could be he's been passed from home to home. Either way, moving into a new household full of strangers will be quite stressful. It's important to be especially patient with your Tibetan Mastiff during this transition period. He may have lapses in his housetraining or be particularly aloof toward certain family members. Patience and understanding will go a long way toward helping your new dog feel comfortable in his new home.

Bringing home an adult dog also means that your new Tibetan Mastiff will have already developed certain habits and preferences. If you have children or other pets at home, it's especially important to ask the breeder or shelter staff about the dog's prior experiences. If you've found your dream dog, you should also be willing to introduce him to all members of the family, both human and animal, before committing to adoption. Even if the shelter staff or breeder claim that the dog is wonderful with kids and pets alike, it's still a good idea to introduce everyone before you bring him home. Introductions done on neutral territory will help prepare both your new dog and your current pets for the stressful transition period to come.

How to Choose your Ideal Dog

Choosing the perfect Tibetan Mastiff can seem like a daunting task, but a knowledgeable breeder or rescue representative can help you make the right decision. As long as you've already discussed your long-term goals, as well as any dealbreakers, you and the breeder or shelter staff member can work together to find your dream dog.

The most important aspect of choosing your ideal dog is to not focus on appearance. It can be easy to become distracted by a cute, fluffy Tibetan Mastiff puppy, but just because you find the puppy's appearance appealing, does not mean he's the right fit for you and your family. You may have a certain color or appearance in mind, but you should keep your mind open to other options as well. Consider the dog's temperament above all else. If you're looking for a future show ring star, you will also need to look for any traits that may disqualify your new dog from competition. Remember, the breeder will have known the puppies from birth and will likely serve as an invaluable resource in choosing the right dog for your lifestyle, so be sure to take their advice into consideration when making your final choice.

CHAPTER 4

Preparing Your Family for a Tibetan Mastiff

Yearly Costs of Owning a Tibetan Mastiff

The first year of Tibetan Mastiff ownership can be quite costly, so it's important to have an accurate understanding of what you may need to spend. If you're living paycheck to paycheck, you may need to seriously reconsider whether bringing a dog into your home is the best decision. However, regardless of your income, with proper planning and preparation, the cost of owning a Tibetan Mastiff can be easily managed.

The initial cost of adopting or buying a Tibetan Mastiff can vary greatly. If you've chosen to adopt your new dog from a shelter or rescue organization, you'll need to pay an adoption fee. Adoption fees can range anywhere from $100 to $500 or more, depending on the organization, the area you live in, and the specific care given to the dog while in the rescue's care. Although this fee can seem steep at times, remember that this money helps cover the cost of the care provided to the dog before your adoption and may also help pay for the care of other animals within their organization. Some organizations also consider adoption fees a tax-deductible donation, so be sure to ask a shelter representative if this is the case. On the bright side, most dogs adopted from a rescue are up to date on vaccines and may have already been spayed or neutered.

HELPFUL TIP
Strong Jaws

Tibetan Mastiffs have incredibly powerful jaws and teeth. Their intelligence and desire to roam a property to protect it can lead to massive amounts of destruction if the dogs are left home alone and are bored all day. The Tibetan Mastiff is not a breed that will happily snooze on the sofa all day.

If you've chosen instead to purchase your Tibetan Mastiff from a breeder, you may be looking at spending anywhere from $1000 to $3500 or more. The price will depend on the individual dog's pedigree, show potential, and breeder's reputation. By the time you bring your new puppy home, it's likely that the breeder has given the litter at least one round of vaccines. If you're adopting an adult from a breeder, the dog may be up to date on vaccines already, so be sure to ask what vet care is necessary after adoption.

However, though the initial cost can be quite expensive, it will unfortunately be the least of your financial concerns. If you own other dogs, you may be able to cut corners with hand-me-downs, but if your new Tibetan Mastiff is your only dog, the cost of supplies can add up quickly. Combined with the cost of routine veterinary care, you may be spending anywhere from $1065 to $3810 during your first year of ownership, not including the initial purchase price or adoption fee. Here's a breakdown of the potential cost of Tibetan Mastiff ownership during your first year:

Mandatory Expenses	Cost Estimate
Food	$300 - $900
Food and Water Dishes	$10 - $50
Treats	$50 - $150
Toys	$20 - $100
Collars and Leashes	$10 - $100
Crate	$50 - $200
Dog Beds	$50 - $350
Vaccines and Routine Veterinary Care	$150 - $500
Heartworm Testing	$10 - $35
Heartworm Prevention	$25 - $125
Flea and Tick Prevention	$40 - $200
Spaying and Neutering	$150 - $600
Puppy Classes	$200 - $500
Total	**$1065 - $3810**

Unfortunately, supplies and routine care are not the only potential costs you need to worry about. If your budget is tight, you may be able to save some money by grooming your Tibetan Mastiff yourself. However, if you intend to have your dog groomed by a professional, you'll need to be prepared to spend $60 to $150 every six to eight weeks. The exact cost will depend on the area you live in as well as the level of service provided by your groomer. Grooming a Tibetan Mastiff can be hard work, so many owners are happy to let a professional handle their dog's grooming needs, but be sure to budget accordingly.

Tibetan Mastiffs are large dogs and can be somewhat difficult to travel with if you don't plan accordingly. If you plan to travel without your beloved companion, you'll need to consider the cost of leaving him

at a boarding facility or hiring a pet sitter. Again, depending on the area you live in and the level of service provided, you may spend upwards of $80 per day. Of course, if you have friends or family members who love dogs, you may be able to ask them to care for your Tibetan Mastiff while you're away.

The biggest expense you may face as a dog owner is emergency veterinary care. Even if you do your best to keep your Tibetan Mastiff safe and healthy, accidents can and do occur. Depending on the severity of the incident, emergency care can range from just a few hundred dollars to several thousand. Investing in pet insurance or setting aside a small monetary amount each month can help you prepare for this potential expense when tragedy strikes.

Possible Expenses	Cost Estimate
Professional Grooming	$150 - $900+
Emergency Veterinary Services	$200 - $2000+
Pet Sitting or Boarding	$15 - $80+ per day

It's important to note that these numbers are not intended to scare you away from Tibetan Mastiff ownership. Rather, it's meant to prepare you for the potential financial burden of caring for a living, breathing animal. Bringing home a new pet is a big responsibility and you need to carefully consider whether you're willing or able to spend the money needed to provide proper care. With careful planning and budgeting, it is feasible to provide the best care possible without causing undue financial hardship.

Preparing Children

Before you bring your Tibetan Mastiff home, it's important to explain to your children how to properly and safely interact with a new dog. In the moment, they may be too excited to listen to you, so you need to sit them down

Photo Courtesy
of Dani Allen Smith

for a discussion prior to the new dog's arrival. You'll need to explain how to gently approach and handle the dog to prevent him from becoming frightened or overwhelmed. You'll also need to explain what to do when the puppy bites or jumps on them. It's important to have a clear idea of the house rules at this point so that you can all agree as a family how to enforce them. It's also a good idea to discourage your children from picking the puppy up to prevent any injuries from dropping.

This is also an ideal opportunity to encourage your kids to pick up after themselves. Puppies are unable to distinguish puppy toys from kids' toys,

Photo Courtesy of Nikki Love

so they're likely to chew on anything they can find. In addition to the frustration caused by having a favorite toy chewed to pieces, chunks of plastic or stuffed toys can easily become a choking hazard or potential gastrointestinal blockage.

You should also discuss any other aspect of the puppy's safety with your kids before picking up your new family member. Be sure to mention the importance

HELPFUL TIP
Good Family Dogs?

While Tibetan Mastiffs can get along quite well with a family's children, they can mistake playing for fighting and may not tolerate children roughhousing with their friends. A Tibetan Mastiff may protect your child a little TOO well and make it hard for anybody to visit your home.

of making sure all doors and gates are latched to prevent a puppy from escaping or simply wandering out an open door. Pools and flights of stairs can be quite dangerous to a young puppy, so be sure to explain the importance of keeping the puppy in his designated area. You may also want to discourage your children from interacting with the puppy without adult supervision to prevent any unnecessary injuries or accidents.

Mutual Respect

When introducing a new dog into your home, it's important that all family members, both human and animal, maintain a certain level of mutual respect. While there are bound to be a few bumps in the road, it's important to make sure everyone is as comfortable as possible. As previously stated, it's important to monitor all interactions between children and the new dog to make sure everyone's personal boundaries are being respected. It can be easy for kids and dogs alike to become overstimulated and act inappropriately but with proper supervision this can be prevented.

If you have other pets in the house, it's important to respect their boundaries as well. Some pets may be unhappy about a new dog in the house, especially if they've been the only animal in the home for some time. You can help each animal maintain their comfort by providing them with a certain safe space. Keeping your puppy in a playpen or designated room while not actively interacting with him can help ensure that your current pets aren't overwhelmed by a rambunctious and playful puppy. Remember, this is a stressful time for everyone so it's important to do what you can to minimize the stress and ease the family through this transition.

Preparing for Mealtime

While it may seem that your dog's mealtime is an uneventful part of the day, it's actually a wonderful opportunity to teach your dog respect and patience. The first step in making the most out of mealtime is to ensure that you're adequately prepared. Before bringing your new Tibetan Mastiff home, make sure you have bowls for both food and water, as well as an adequate amount of appropriate food. Remember, it's best to start with whatever type of food the breeder or shelter was feeding your dog and to slowly transition the dog to your food of choice. This slow transition can help ease any gastrointestinal issues that may occur if the diet is changed too quickly.

You should also decide with your family what time your new Tibetan Mastiff will be fed, who will feed him, and how you will now if he's been fed already. It's not uncommon for dogs to be fed dinner more than once in a busy household, so make a plan and commit to it. Many families create a sign or place the food or bowls in different locations to indicate whether the dog has been fed. Although an occasional extra meal is unlikely to have any long-term effect, excess calories on a regular basis can be problematic for your dog's health and waistline.

Playtime with Your Tibetan Mastiff

When playing with your new Tibetan Mastiff, it's essential that you discourage rough play. With large breeds, rough play can lead to humans getting knocked over and possibly injured. Puppies also tend to bite during play, so you'll need to discourage this to prevent any of your family members from getting injured accidentally. Additionally, rough play can escalate quickly between dogs, so if your Tibetan Mastiff engages in play with your other dogs, you should monitor closely and discourage it if it gets too rough. Although Tibetan Mastiffs can easily learn the meaning of the word "no", they may be too focused on their game to listen. Some owners have found success in spritzing their dogs in the face with a spray bottle filled with water to encourage them to listen. The water won't hurt the dog, but it's an unpleasant sensation that usually makes him pay attention. If the play session is between your new dog and children, you may need to remind them regularly to play gently.

As far as toys go, there is no single type of toy that will appeal to all dogs. Most types of toys can be easily destroyed by a Tibetan Mastiff's strong jaws, so choose carefully. It should be noted that Tibetan Mastiffs rarely enjoy structured games such as fetch or chasing a frisbee, so you may need to experiment to see what type of play your dog prefers. Some dogs may not show any interest in toys, preferring instead to wrestle and chase other dogs or family members.

Preparing Your Other Pets

Before you bring your new Tibetan Mastiff home for the first time, it's important to have a plan to introduce him to your other pets. This is especially important if you plan on bringing home an adult. Some Tibetan Mastiffs can be aggressive or overly dominant toward other dogs and pets, so take this into consideration when choosing your new dog. If you have other dominant dogs in your home already, a Tibetan Mastiff may not be your first choice. However, if you do believe a Tibetan Mastiff is the right breed for you, consider introducing your new dog to your existing pets somewhere other than your home. Introductions done on neutral territory are more likely to succeed since neither animal will feel the need to protect his property or home.

Some Tibetan Mastiffs may also have a strong prey drive, so use caution when introducing your new dog to smaller pets. Small dogs, cats, and even poultry can trigger a dog's prey drive, so be sure to monitor any interaction between your Tibetan Mastiff and your small pets until you know whether they can be trusted together. In the beginning, you may need to guide your Tibetan Mastiff through these interactions and let him know that aggression is not acceptable. However, you should also be prepared to accept the fact that some dogs with high prey drive can never be trusted around small animals and will always need to be separated from them or monitored closely.

It's entirely possible that your current pets may not get along with your new Tibetan Mastiff right away. If this happens, you need to be patient as some pets may need more time to adjust to changes in their home. Introducing a new family member can be upsetting, particularly if a pet is older. You may need to introduce them slowly over a period of days or even weeks before they get along. Patience is key in these situations, as rushing can cause further stress and setbacks. Until your pets decide to be friendly with each other, you must also be willing to keep them separated if necessary, to prevent any accidents or injuries from occurring. Slow introductions can seem like a hassle, but it's essential that you take the time needed to set your pets up for a healthy and happy lifelong relationship.

Family Commitment

Adopting a Tibetan Mastiff is a huge commitment and you need to be sure that all family members are ready for the responsibility. Caring for and training puppies requires a lot of time and energy from everyone involved. Likewise, adopting an adult will go much more smoothly if everyone does their share of the work. Before committing to an adoption or signing any contract, sit down with your family to make sure everyone is on the same page.

Tibetan Mastiffs are not a breed that can be stuck in the backyard and forgotten. They require constant training and socialization, or they may be-

Photo Courtesy of Maria Johansson

come aggressive and unmanageable. An aggressive dog can be a liability to not only your neighbors, but your own family. Serious injuries are certain to occur if an unsocialized or aggressive Tibetan Mastiff feels pressured to protect his property. To prevent tragedy, you need to make sure your entire family is ready for the responsibility of Tibetan Mastiff ownership. This is not a decision to be taken lightly. Tibetan Mastiffs can make wonderful, loving family companions, but each and every family member must stay committed to this goal.

CHAPTER 5
Preparing Your Home for Your New Tibetan Mastiff

"Space and fences are your best friends. A quarter acre lot is big enough for a male/female pair. Smaller might work with a single TM and one or two other dogs of less demanding breeds. TMs are not apartment dogs unless you get an older well civilized retiree and live on the first floor. As you add more space you can have more dogs. "

Dr. Charles Radcliffe
Timberline Tibetan Mastiffs

*Photo Courtesy of
Richard Eichhorn & Efrain Valle
Drakyi Tibetan Mastiffs*

Drakyi Goddess of Love, VENUS

Creating a Safe Area Indoors

"A TM puppy will explore and get into anything and everything so I do not recommend just giving a puppy free run of the house. We start out with an exercise pen with puppy pads, and frequent walks outside, and early crate training as a crate is like a safe den to dogs and gives them a place to relax."

Michael Brantley
Dreamland Kennel

Before allowing your new Tibetan Mastiff access to your home, you need to make sure it's free of obvious dangers. Electrical cords are some of the biggest dangers facing curious puppies. Remember, puppies do not have hands, so they explore the world through their mouth. A puppy can quickly and easily chew through an electrical cord before you have the opportunity to take it away from him. To prevent this type of accident, try to pick up any electrical cords off the floor or protect them from puppy teeth with durable covers.

It's also essential that you make sure all cleaning products, pest control products, and other household chemicals are kept out of your new dog's reach. A curious Tibetan Mastiff exploring his new home can easily get into trouble if these types of products are left out. Medication, beauty, and hygiene products can also pose a threat to dogs if ingested, so you may want to consider installing cabinet locks designed for toddlers if you can't set these products up out of your dog's reach.

Stairs can also pose a threat to your new family member, particularly if you've chosen to bring home a puppy or a senior dog. Puppies and older dogs often lack the strength and coordination required to navigate long flights of stairs and can be seriously injured if they fall. If your home has anything more than a few steps at a time, consider installing a pressure-mounted baby gate or other barrier to prevent your Tibetan Mastiff from accidentally tumbling down the stairs.

Although it may seem innocuous, trashcans can be incredibly dangerous for dogs. Trashcans often contain a variety of hazards from toxic food to broken dishes to old batteries. A bored or curious Tibetan Mastiff can easily knock over a trashcan to explore its contents, so you must ensure that all trash is safely protected. If you can't store your trashcan in a cabinet or closet, consider investing in one with a locking lid. This is a common problem with dogs of all breeds so there are many trashcans on the market designed to keep curious pets and neighborhood pests out.

Outdoor Dangers

As you puppy proof your home, don't forget to check your outdoor spaces for potential dangers. Just as you did with your indoor spaces, it can be helpful to get down on the ground and look at your yard or garden from your Tibetan Mastiff's perspective. Be sure to walk along every inch of your fence to look for any holes, loose boards, or other ways your dog could escape. A canine escapee can be exposed to many dangers outside your home such as cars, wild animals, and even humans with ill intent. To prevent tragedy, it's crucial that you make sure your yard is completely secure before you allow your new family member to explore his new outdoor space.

As you walk around your yard or garden, you should also go over the types of plants that are growing there. Be on the lookout for any toxic plants that your new Tibetan Mastiff could ingest. Again, puppies are incredibly curious and will stick anything in their mouth, so if you find any toxic plants, you'll need to either remove them or build a barrier around them. Common outdoor plants that are toxic to dogs include hemlock, English ivy, mistletoe, and amaryllis. If you're unsure of whether a plant is safe, the AKC has a list of poisonous plants published on their website or you can ask your veterinarian.

If your yard has a pool, you'll need to make sure there's no way your Tibetan Mastiff can access it without supervision. Even if your dog is a fan of swimming, if he finds himself suddenly in water he may panic and not be able to find his way out. To prevent tragedy, make sure your pool is completely surrounded and that your dog cannot squeeze through any gaps in the fencing. If the gaps in your fence are too large, consider lining the bottom half of the fence with chicken wire or garden fencing. Most dogs won't chew on this type of fencing so it should discourage your dog from trying to break through. If your pool is not fenced, you'll need to make sure that your dog is never allowed in the area unless he is closely supervised. Accidental drowning is a preventable accident, so make sure you do what you can to keep your dog safe.

*Photo Courtesy
of Maureen McCulloch*

Supplies

Before you bring your Tibetan Mastiff home, you should try to make a list of the supplies you'll need. Making a list and checking it at least twice will help prevent any last minute panic when you realize you forgot to buy a crate. If you have other dogs in your home, you may have most or all the supplies, but it can still be helpful to see a reminder of what you may need. Even if you already have everything, you may want to buy duplicates in case your other dogs have trouble sharing.

The most important item on your list should be puppy food. You don't want to get your puppy home and realize you have nothing to feed him. Before picking up your new Tibetan Mastiff, ask the breeder or shelter representative what type of food your dog is currently eating. Even if you don't plan on feeding that type of food long-term, you'll need to pick up a small amount so that you can safely transition your dog onto the food of your choice. Dietary changes done slowly over a period of several days to a week are less likely to cause digestive upset. This is also a good time to ask about any dietary sensitivities or allergies. If your dog is sensitive to a certain ingredient, you'll want to know so that you can avoid it in both food and treats. Speaking of treats, training should begin as soon as you bring your Tibetan Mastiff home, so pick up some high value treats to encourage your dog to learn the rules of the house. Treats that are small and easy to eat work best for training.

Don't forget to get your Tibetan Mastiff an appropriately sized collar and leash. Most collars are adjustable, so if you aren't sure about the size of your dog's neck you should be able to estimate. Remember, Tibetan Mastiffs have a lot of coat around their necks, so you want to make sure you find a collar that's tight enough not to slide off, but not so tight that it causes discomfort. You also want to choose a collar that won't cause matting or hair breakage. Richard Eichhorn of Drakyi Tibetan Mastiffs recommends rolled leather or nylon collars or serpentine style metal choke collars, as they tend to sit between the layers of coat, rather than on top. Your local pet store or favorite online retailer will likely have a huge array of colors and styles so you should be able to find one that appeals to you no matter your taste.

HELPFUL TIP
Not for Everyone

Tibetan Mastiffs aren't appropriate dogs for everyone thanks to their size, stubbornness, and tendency to become aggressive in the wrong hands. Only experienced dog owners who know how to handle large dogs should tackle the Tibetan Mastiff.

Photo Courtesy of Nikki Love

Most collars will have matching leashes available, but when choosing a leash, you need to keep your dog's size in mind. Dainty leads may look nice, but you don't want one to break the first time your Tibetan Mastiff lunges at a passing squirrel. Be sure to pick up an identification tag with your current phone number or address as well. If your new dog manages to escape your home, you want to make sure he's able to find his way back to you.

While shopping for your new Tibetan Mastiff, you'll need to decide what type of bed he might prefer. Dogs beds come in a wide variety of shapes, sizes, and styles, so you might want to consider whether your dog prefers to sleep curled up or lying flat. Most importantly, try to find a bed with a removable and washable cover. You may need to wash the entire bed at times, but if it's only a surface stain it would be much easier to just wash the cover. You might also want to look for beds made out of more durable fabrics as many Tibetan Mastiffs may view their new bed as a chew toy, rather than something comfortable to sleep on. With large breed dogs, such as Tibetan Mastiffs, many owners find that thicker beds or ones made of memory foam are easier on a dog's joints, especially as he ages. However, as Tibetan Mastiffs have such heavy coats, they often prefer sleeping on cold tile or cement floors, rather than cushy beds.

If you would like to purchase toys for your new Tibetan Mastiff, it's important to remember that Tibetan Mastiffs are known for their ability to chew through nearly anything. Many owners have been disappointed to learn that their furniture is no match for their Tibetan Mastiff's teeth. It can be helpful to provide your new dog with toys to chew on, rather than your sofa, but keep a close eye on him while he's chewing. If you notice any small pieces have been chewed off or the toy has been chewed down to a size that could be swallowed, dispose of the toy immediately. It's cheaper to toss the toy in the trash and buy a new one than it is to have the toy surgically removed from your dog's digestive track. There are many types of toys on the market designed for dogs with powerful jaws, so consider trying a few out to see if they might last a bit longer than normal dog toys.

FUN FACT

Lhasa Apso Pals

While Tibetan Mastiffs are natural guard dogs, they aren't as observant as the much smaller Lhasa Apso. In Tibet, the two dog breeds are often kept together, and the Lhasa will alert the Tibetan to approaching strangers.

Regardless of whether you plan on having a professional groom your Tibetan Mastiff, you may want to have a few grooming tools on hand to keep your new dog looking and smelling fresh between grooming appointments. Tibetan Mastiffs have a lot of coat, so you'll likely need to do some brushing at home. Slicker brushes work well, but often don't reach far through thick coats, so metal rake brushes are recommended. Combs are also an excellent way to make sure that you're brushing the entire coat, not just the surface layer. You might consider purchasing shampoo or conditioner to have at home in case your puppy rolls in something smelly. If you plan on trimming your dog's nails yourself, you'll want to invest in a high-quality nail trimmer. If you're unsure of what type of product will work best with your Tibetan Mastiff, don't be afraid to ask your local groomer for advice.

Regardless of whether you're bringing home a puppy or an adult Tibetan Mastiff, it's a good idea to pick up a few housetraining supplies. Even adults can have accidents when put into stressful situations, so it's best to be prepared just in case. Most pet stores or online retailers have both disposable and reusable puppy pads, both work well in aiding with cleanup. Cleaning supplies will also be an essential part of your housetraining toolbox. Cleaners designed specifically for pet messes often contain certain enzymes designed to eliminate odor and discourage future messes. You can even buy bells to hang on your door so that your dog can let you know when he needs to go outside by pawing or nudging at the bells. Most importantly, don't forget to buy a crate so that you can begin crate training immediately.

Basic Shopping List for Your New Tibetan Mastiff

- Collar and leash
- Identification tag
- Crate
- Bedding
- Food
- Treats
- Toys
- Combs or brushes
- Shampoo
- Nail trimmer
- Puppy pads
- Cleaning supplies

Setting Up Your Dog's Personal Space

Once you've puppy-proofed the indoors and outdoors, and have purchased supplies, you can decide where your new puppy is going to live for the first few weeks or months. Limiting your new dog's access to your home until you're more certain of his level of training will help reduce the likelihood of housetraining accidents and precious items getting chewed up. Many owners opt to keep their new dogs in a laundry room, guest bathroom, or a corner of the kitchen. Choosing a smaller space can help your dog with housetraining, as dogs don't like to relieve themselves too close the areas in which they eat and sleep. Regardless of the size of the space you choose, try to choose an area with flooring that will be easy to clean, such as tile or linoleum. If possible, it's also ideal to choose a room where your new dog will be able to watch your family activities without feeling isolated.

You'll also need to make sure your new Tibetan Mastiff won't be able to escape his designated area. Although Tibetan Mastiffs don't typically try to jump over barriers, their size and weight can easily knock down flimsy baby gates or barriers. Make sure all pressure-mounted baby gates or freestanding barriers are installed correctly to prevent an escape or injury to your new family member.

After you're certain that the area is safe, you can begin setting up your Tibetan Mastiff's supplies. Start by laying out a few disposable or reusable puppy pads. Absorbent pads will make cleaning up after the inevitable housetraining accidents a breeze. It's much easier to pick up a pad and either throw it away or wash it than it is to scrub floors while trying to keep an overly enthusiastic puppy at bay. You might also consider placing one of these pads under your dog's food and water dishes to prevent any unnecessary messes. It's important to note that puppy pads can be dangerous if ingested, so if you notice your Tibetan Mastiff chewing on them, you may need to take them away and do without. It may be inconvenient to constantly clean your floors, but it's better that a potential tragedy and the vet bills that come with it.

When planning out your new dog's space, you may also want to consider putting his bedding near the entrance to the area. The entryway is likely where your dog will be waiting for you or watching the family go about their daily activities so it can be helpful to make sure he's comfortable. Even though Tibetan Mastiffs have plenty of hair to keep them warm, some enjoy snuggling with blankets, so consider giving your dog a small blanket to cuddle with. As with all items in your puppy's area, if you notice any chewing, remove the bedding immediately. Many Tibetan Mastiffs will enthusiastically shred their brand new beds and rip out the stuffing just because they can. The stuffing and shredded fabric can easily become a choking hazard or potential intestinal blockage. There are many beds on the market these days that are advertised as being tougher than most materials. Unfortunately, few beds are a match for the powerful jaws of a Tibetan Mastiff, but if you can discourage the chewing, these tougher beds might last a bit longer than most.

It's best to place your Tibetan Mastiff's food and water bowls in a quiet back corner of your dog's space. It may be more convenient to be able to monitor your dog's food and water intake when the bowls are placed up front, but an excited puppy can more easily knock them over in this location. By placing them in a less heavily trafficked area of the space, you reduce the chances of a mess. You should also try to keep the food and water some distance away from your Tibetan Mastiff's bedding to prevent it from getting wet or soiled from a spill. Just remember to keep a close eye on your dog's dishes to ensure that he has access to clean water at all times.

Crates and Crate Training

Regardless of age, crate training is an essential part of your Tibetan Mastiff's education. However, it's important that your dog comes to enjoy his time there, rather than seeing it as a punishment. Richard Eichhorn of Drakyi Tibetan Mastiffs advises, "You and your dog need to learn at an early age that the crate is a home away from home, but is not a cage to be used for confinement. It can and should become a convenient, safe haven for your dog in the home, in the car, at a dog show, and while on vacation. From the puppy stage on, the crate, or the 'den' can be used as the bed and as an aid in housebreaking, and rewards should be given to encourage its use." Additionally, if your dog spends any time at the vet or groomer, crate training will be necessary for your dog's safety.

Dogs who have not been properly crate trained often panic once they're enclosed. Rather than walking into the crate politely, they end up having to be forced inside, which is never advisable. In particular, this type of force rarely ends well with Tibetan Mastiffs. Incessant barking and digging or chewing at the crate door are common in dogs who are unused to spending time in a crate. They may also relieve themselves out of stress. Not only is it a stressful experience for those caring for such a dog, but there is a high risk of the dog injuring his paws or teeth in his attempts to escape. To prevent any unnecessary stress or injury, it's crucial that you teach your Tibetan Mastiff that the crate is a safe and comfortable place for him.

Before you begin training, you need to decide what type of crate to use. Crates can be made out of a variety of materials including wood, metal, and plastic. Some are designed to stylishly blend with your décor, while others may be more simplistic or designed for use with particularly destructive dogs. They also vary greatly in cost. Metal wire crates and airline-approved plastic crates tend to be far less expensive than heavy-duty metal panel and fashionable wooden crates. The type of crate you choose will depend on your own taste as well as your budget.

Regardless of material, it's important to make sure the crate is big enough for your dog, but not so large that he feels comfortable relieving himself inside. The crate should be large enough for your dog to stand up, turn around, and lie down comfortably. If you've decided to bring home a puppy, you'll need to adjust his crate size as he grows. This can be accomplished either by using inexpensive crates that you can replace as he grows or investing in a wire crate with a moveable divider. Crates with dividers allow you to purchase one crate, usually in a size appropriate for an adult Tibetan Mastiff, and adjust the space available to your dog as he grows. As an adult, your Tibetan Mastiff will likely need a crate designed specifically for giant breed dogs.

Once you have an appropriate-sized crate, you should try to make it as appealing as possible to encourage your dog to spend time in it. Make sure it's comfortable by placing his favorite bed or blankets inside. If he has a favorite toy, you might try tossing it inside to entice him. However, it's best not to leave toys inside the crate if you don't plan on supervising your dog. The powerful jaws of a Tibetan Mastiff can chew up a toy in minutes, potentially leading to ingested toy parts. This rule also applies to bedding. If your dog is a chewer, you may need to remove his bedding while he's in the crate without supervision. As your dog gains experience with the crate, you may be able to reintroduce bedding at your own discretion.

To get your Tibetan Mastiff comfortable with the crate, encourage him to step inside on his own by tossing a few treats inside. Remember, Tibetan Mastiffs prefer to do things their own way so your training will be most successful if you can convince your dog that going in the crate was his idea rather than yours. Once he becomes comfortable going in and out of the crate on his own, you can begin to shut the door behind him. Start with only a few seconds at a time and be sure to reward him accordingly. Slowly, you can increase the amount of time you leave the door shut and even begin stepping away from the crate. If your Tibetan Mastiff gets upset while inside the crate, it's important to allow him to calm down before releasing him. If you release him as soon as he starts to bark or cry, you're only teaching him that throwing a tantrum will get him out of the situation. With enough patience and encouragement, your dog will soon come to enjoy the peace and quiet of his crate.

The Importance of Having a Plan

Thoroughly planning your Tibetan Mastiff's arrival will make the transition into your home less stressful for both you and your new family member. Bringing a new dog into your home without any planning at all will result in chaos and panic, which can be an overwhelming start to this new relationship. By planning everything out, from the ride home to the space you'll be keeping your new dog, you'll hopefully be able to introduce your Tibetan Mastiff to your home with minimal stress and leave him with a positive impression of your home and family.

For some families, especially those with no other dogs in the home, it can be helpful to sit down and discuss the rules of the house prior to bringing your new Tibetan Mastiff home. Setting up clear rules and deciding the best way to enforce these rules will ensure that all family members are on the same page. Topics you might want to discuss with your family include whether the dog will be allowed on the furniture, where he will sleep and eat, and how to properly greet new people.

If you have other dogs, you may be more prepared for potential problems with a new dog's arrival simply because you've had experience with this situation in the past. However, if it has been some time since you've welcomed a new dog into your home, you can certainly benefit from developing a plan before you pick your Tibetan Mastiff up. Some owners even choose to write everything down, as having a visual representation in front of them can help ensure the plan's success. Having a written plan will give you a resource to refer to when things go awry. Bringing a new dog into your household can be incredibly stressful and it can be easy to forget things if you don't have them written down.

Developing a Schedule

Before your first day at home with your new Tibetan Mastiff, sit down and picture what an average day in your household will look like. Consider what time you wake up in the morning and how much time you have before your family needs to leave for work or school. Ask yourself how flexible your workday is and if you are able to leave at lunchtime to check on your puppy. You'll also want to consider what time each family member gets home in the evenings and whether that changes based on the day of the week. By working out a clear picture of your family's schedule, you'll be better able to work a new dog's needs into your daily routine. Remember, the more consistent you can be with your Tibetan Mastiff's schedule, the more quickly he'll be able to adapt to life in your home.

When working out a possible schedule for your new Tibetan Mastiff, it's important to sit all members of the family down to decide who will help with the responsibilities of dog ownership. Particularly young children may not be able to help much, but older children can certainly help care for a new dog. For some families, it can be helpful to assign certain tasks to each family member to ensure that they are done correctly. Without discussion, it's possible that someone may forget to feed or walk the dog, or he may get fed multiple dinners. This lack of communication isn't the end of the world, but it will make it more difficult for your dog to get used to life with your family. Like weekly chores, some households find it helpful to write out a list of dog-related chores and assign each chore to a family member who must then check it off the list once completed. No matter what it takes to accomplish a consistent schedule, you must be willing to put in the extra effort to help your Tibetan Mastiff's transition into your home go as smoothly as possible

CHAPTER 6
Bringing Your New Tibetan Mastiff Home

Picking Your Dog Up from the Breeder or Shelter

The day you pick your new Tibetan Mastiff up from the breeder or shelter can be both exciting and overwhelming. Before you leave to pick up your new family member, be sure to double check your home to make sure that you're thoroughly prepared for the arrival. Go through your new dog's designated area one last time to make sure it's completely puppy proofed. You should also go through your supply list one last time to make sure you have everything you need. It can be a pain to have to run out for supplies after getting your puppy home, so make sure you're as prepared as possible. If you do need to pick up a few last-minute supplies, be sure to do so on the way to the shelter or breeder, rather than on the way home. If

you stop on the way home, you will either need to leave your new dog in the car or take him into the store with you. Both can be incredibly stressful for a dog who has just left his littermates for the first time in his life. Additionally, taking an unvaccinated or under-vaccinated puppy into a store puts your new family member's health at risk. You want your puppy's introduction into your home to be as stress free as possible, so try to make the trip home with as few stops as possible.

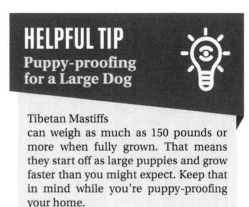

HELPFUL TIP
Puppy-proofing for a Large Dog

Tibetan Mastiffs can weigh as much as 150 pounds or more when fully grown. That means they start off as large puppies and grow faster than you might expect. Keep that in mind while you're puppy-proofing your home.

Again, it's helpful to have everything prepared before you pick up your Tibetan Mastiff, so if you've already received a copy of the breeder's contract or the shelter's adoption agreement, try to read through it beforehand if possible. This way, you can think of any questions you may have about the document and what you're agreeing to. Some breeders may require a deposit to hold your puppy until he's ready to go home, so if you've already paid the deposit, make sure this is documented in the contract as well as the amount that will be paid upon pickup. Remember, the contract is a legally binding document, so you want to make sure that you look over it thoroughly and are aware of what you're agreeing to. If you've chosen to adopt from a shelter, you'll likely need to sign an adoption agreement. This agreement is similar to a breeder's contract and is meant to prioritize the wellbeing of the dog while protecting both the shelter and adopter.

Along with any questions you may have about the contract or adoption agreement, be sure to make a list of any questions you have about your new Tibetan Mastiff. Perhaps you have questions about the breed itself or about how to connect with other Tibetan Mastiff owners. No matter what your question may entail, it's better to ask now than to regret not asking at all. If your excitement over bringing your new family member home distracts you from asking questions, don't fret. Most breeders and shelter staff members are happy to maintain contact down the road, so if you think of any questions after getting your puppy home, you can always contact them later.

The Ride Home

The drive from the breeder's home or the shelter to your own home may not seem like a noteworthy event, but you need to consider the fact that this may be your Tibetan Mastiff's first time in the car. He's likely going to be riding in the car fairly often throughout his life, so it's important to leave a positive impression on him. The most important aspect of the ride home is remaining calm throughout the drive. A nervous puppy may not understand that your excitement and elevated emotions are due to him and not due to the car ride. This can lead to anxiety and even panic.

Regardless of your new Tibetan Mastiff's previous experience riding in cars, you'll need to keep him restrained for the duration of the trip. Depending on the age and size of your new companion, you may want to explore different restraint options. Older, experienced canine travelers may be comfortable in a harness and seat belt or behind a barrier. Younger or more inexperienced dogs may prefer the comforting confinement of a crate. Many dogs find the security of a crate to be comforting, so you may want to try this method for the first few trips. You can also cover the crate with a blanket or towel if you feel that your dog needs a more enclosed space to feel safe. You'll also need to consider the type of vehicle you drive when deciding which type of restraint works best for you. Some cars or smaller vehicles may not be able to fit a crate large enough for an adult Tibetan Mastiff. If this is the case, you may need to use doggy seatbelts or barriers instead. Unrestrained dogs are an accident waiting to happen, so to ensure that all members of your family make it home safe, be sure to keep your new dog restrained until you're safely in your own driveway.

It's also important to be prepared for any potential carsickness with your Tibetan Mastiff. Even experienced adult dogs can become sick on occasion, so it's best to be prepared just in case. Depending on the method of restraint you've chosen, you may want to consider investing in car seat covers or bringing along a few towels or puppy pads. Lining a crate with something you can either wash or dispose of will help with cleanup if your new dog does get sick on the way home. If you have a long drive ahead of you, you may also want to bring a plastic bag to store any soiled linens in case you need to replace them with clean ones.

Depending on your Tibetan Mastiff's previous experience in cars, you should be prepared for anything as some dogs react badly their first few times in car. Cars can be scary for a nervous dog and he may cry, bark, or even try to escape. This is another reason why restraints are so important. Remember, no matter how upset your dog gets, you must remain as calm as possible. If you get upset too, he'll only believe that there's a reason to panic. Instead, by remaining calm you'll let him know that there's nothing to worry about and that you have everything under control. If possible, consider bringing a blanket or toy along from the breeder's home or the shelter as a familiar scent may provide your dog with some comfort.

Photo Courtesy of Melissa McKiddy

Introducing Your Tibetan Mastiff to Your Other Pets

If you have other pets in your home, you will need to introduce them to your new Tibetan Mastiff in an area that your current pets will consider as neutral territory. This can be difficult with a puppy who hasn't yet received his full schedule of vaccinations, but even the front yard or an infrequently used guest room will work fine. As long as your current pets do not spend a significant amount of time in the area, it should work for introductions.

It's best to do all initial introduction with both your Tibetan Mastiff and your current pets being restrained. Remember, an excitable puppy or new dog can be overwhelming to a pet that has gotten used to its current lifestyle, so you want to make sure you can separate them quickly if you need to. A harness and leash are great options for restraint as you'll be able to pull the animals apart in an emergency without hurting them as you might with a collar.

If you have multiple pets in your home already, introduce them to the new dog one at a time. Introducing them as a pack may encourage them to bully your new Tibetan Mastiff and scare him. Allow the animals to view each other from afar at first, either across the room or across the yard. At this point, if either animal shows signs of stress or anxiety, give them time to relax before bringing them closer. If both animals seem comfortable, you can allow them to come closer and even sniff each other. Richard Eichhorn of Drakyi Tibetan Mastiffs recommends sitting on the floor with the puppy and your other animals to help put them both at ease.

Regardless of how well your pets seem to be getting along at first, it's crucial that you never leave them unsupervised during the first few weeks or months together. Accidents can happen quickly and with little warning, so to prevent any injuries or tragedies, it's best to supervise them at all times. While supervising, you must always monitor their body language for signs of discomfort, fear, or stress. It's possible that you may only be able to let your pets interact for a few minutes at a time for the first few days, but this is fine. Go as slowly as you need to in order to ensure your pets are getting along. As tempting as it may be, never rush introductions. If you go too quickly and frighten your pets, you'll start their relationship with a negative impression of each other. You'll then need to work even harder with their training to repair the initial damage, which could have been avoided in the first place.

Introducing Your Tibetan Mastiff to Your Children

Before bringing your Tibetan Mastiff home, it's recommended to have a discussion with your kids to explain how to properly interact with the new dog when he arrives. Trying to explain the rules to your kids with a fluffy new dog in front of them will not work, so it's never a good idea to bring a puppy home as a surprise. Dogs are a big responsibility, even for children, so you want to make sure they're prepared.

If you have other pets in the home, your children may already understand the basic rules of interacting with a dog. However, if your Tibetan Mastiff will be an only pet, you'll need to teach your kids how to properly pet and play with a dog. Young children often have a difficult time understand that they can't treat the new dog like they treat their stuffed animals and that they can hurt a real pet. Teach them to approach the dog slowly and use a gentle touch when petting him. You'll also need to explain that they should never climb or sit on the new dog as they may hurt him. They should be discouraged from picking the puppy up, as even a small fall can seriously injure a puppy. Encourage them to as calm and gentle as possible while interacting with the new dog, regardless of whether it's an adult or puppy.

As with introducing your Tibetan Mastiff to other pets, you'll need to go slowly with children as well. Both kids and dogs can easily become too ex-

Photo Courtesy of Nousis Xaralampos

cited and things can escalate quickly, so it's best that they are only allowed to interact under strict supervision. You'll need to explain to your kids that they can only play with the new dog with an adult in the room and that if the dog is in his crate or designated area he should be left alone. Again, you'll need to monitor the situation for signs of fear or anxiety in both the dog and the children. If anyone seems uncomfortable, separate them immediately. Exuberant puppies and kids can be overwhelming to each other, so don't be afraid to end the session early and try again later. As their relationship develops, you'll be able to let them interact for longer periods of time, but it's best not to allow them unsupervised access to each other until you're certain that both the kids and the dog understand the rules.

Photo Courtesy
of Kellie Akerman

The First Night

Your Tibetan Mastiff's first night in his new home will likely be a sleepless one, so it's best if you can bring your new family member home when you don't have any early appointments the following morning. Regardless of whether you've brought home and adult or a puppy, this is a stressful time in your dog's life, and he may be upset. Adult dogs may have gotten attached to their previously family so they may not understand why they've been taken away. If you've adopted a puppy, this may be his first time away from his mother and littermates, so you can understand why he may be distressed.

It might be tempting to have your new Tibetan Mastiff spend his first night somewhere out of earshot so that you can get a restful night's sleep, but the isolation will only cause fear and anxiety. Instead, allow your dog to sleep as close to you as he can. Until he's been properly housetrained, you may not want him in bed with you, but you can bring his crate into your bedroom. As long as he knows you're nearby, he'll be more comfortable.

Be sure to take your new Tibetan Mastiff out as late as possible for his last bathroom break before bed. Depending on his age and where he's at in housetraining, you may still be up several times during the night but taking him out late will help you get a little sleep before your next trip outside. Remember, a young puppy will need to go out every two to four hours during the night, so be prepared to be up a lot during the first few weeks and months with your new Tibetan Mastiff.

It can be difficult at first to determine the difference between cries for attention and cries to go outside. However, if you know your Tibetan Mastiff relieved himself just an hour or two ago, you can be sure that he's only crying for attention. If this is the case, you'll need to do your best to ignore him. It can be difficult to ignore a crying puppy, but the more you react, the more he'll howl for your attention. If he understands that throwing a tantrum won't get him attention, he'll eventually settle down and realize that it's time to sleep. However, if he starts crying again a few hours later, it's fairly safe to assume that he needs to go to the bathroom so it's best to take him outside as soon as possible.

CHAPTER 7
The First Few Weeks

Standing by Your Expectations

During the first few weeks with your new Tibetan Mastiff, you need to be realistic about your expectations. Bringing home a new dog, either a puppy or an adult, will require a lot of commitment from you and all of your family members. Raising a dog requires a significant amount of time and effort and if you aren't willing to put in either, you can't expect to make any progress in your dog's training. If you only dedicate one 30-minute period per week to your dog's training, you're unlikely to make significant progress and instead may even encounter resistance.

This is not to say that you should spend every minute of every day training your Tibetan Mastiff. Remember, Tibetan Mastiffs rarely respond well to repetitive training. Introducing a new dog into your household will be stressful for everyone involved, so don't start a full-time training schedule the moment you get home. Instead, schedule time for short but frequent training sessions throughout the day. Several five-minute sessions per day will be enough to introduce your Tibetan Mastiff to the concepts you're introducing, but not enough to overwhelm him during this stressful transition period. The quality of the time you spend with your dog should always outweigh the quantity. You want to make the most out of each training session without causing your Tibetan Mastiff to become frustrated. Rather than immediately trying to teach your dog formal obedience, which Tibetan Mastiffs do not excel in anyway, consider starting with basic household rules and manners. Remember, moving into a new household is a stressful event for a dog, so you want to keep your expectations low but remain consistent in your training.

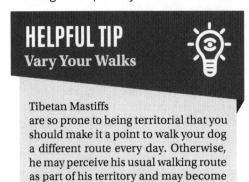

HELPFUL TIP
Vary Your Walks

Tibetan Mastiffs are so prone to being territorial that you should make it a point to walk your dog a different route every day. Otherwise, he may perceive his usual walking route as part of his territory and may become over-protective while being walked through that area.

Establishing Household Rules

"Stay consistent from day one with your goals and expectations. They need a constant routine until they've got the basics figured out."

Jason Phipps
Rare Breed Exotics

During the first few weeks with your new dog, you'll likely run into situations where you'll need to decide as a family on how to handle, but discussing the basic manners expected in your household will be a good start.

One behavior that should be enforced from the moment you bring your dog home is allowing humans to go through a doorway first. It's inappropriate for a dog to shove his way through a door before his human goes through and you'll want to discourage this type of behavior from the start. This is because not only is there a risk of the human getting knocked over, particularly children or older adults, but your dog may try to escape the house by shoving his way out the front door. Instead, encourage your dog to wait patiently any time you take him outside or from room to room. Ask him to sit or stand while you go through and then invite him to come along once you're on the other side of the doorway. With practice and plenty of praise, your Tibetan Mastiff will soon learn that he's expected to wait patiently for an invitation rather that force his way out the door.

Another important opportunity to teach your Tibetan Mastiff proper manners and patience will occur during mealtime. When you serve your new dog his dinner, he should wait patiently for you to place the bowl on the ground. Dogs who do not respect this rule may jump on you, try to knock the bowl out of your hand, or start eating while you're still holding the bowl. To discourage this behavior, ask your dog to sit or stand politely while you set the bowl down. If he attempts to dive at the bowl, tell him 'no' in a firm voice and start from the beginning. Once he's waiting politely, you can set the bowl down and release him. Dogs that are particularly food driven may take some time to learn this behavior, but with practice and consistency, you'll be able to feed your Tibetan Mastiff without any unnecessary excitement or drama.

Another important indicator of a polite and respectful indoor dog is a willingness to move out of the way when asked. Tibetan Mastiffs can be stubborn, so you may need to be firm in your requests during the beginning, but this is an essential skill that all dogs should understand. Whether you're asking your dog to get off the sofa when you ask or simply move out of the way as you clean the floors, he should move when you ask without any attitude or aggression. To accomplish this, you may need to physically move your dog out of the way and there are several ways to do this. You can leave a short leash on your dog until he understands what you're asking and gently pull him in the direction you want him to go or you can gently push him off the furniture or out of the way with your hand. If your Tibetan Mastiff is unfamiliar with this rule, you'll want to use caution as some dogs may try to bite when pushed. You'll also want to avoid grabbing your dog by the collar to pull him off as this places your hand too close to his mouth should he decide to disagree with you. Once your dog has moved out of the way, be sure to praise him enthusiastically to let him know he's done the right thing. With repetition, your Tibetan Mastiff will come to understand that he's expected to move when asked and even if you have to push or pull him at times, he should do so willingly and without an aggressive reaction.

Puppy Problems

When raising a Tibetan Mastiff puppy, you're guaranteed to run into challenges. While it's always possible to correct bad behaviors, it's best to set your dog up for success and do what you can to prevent bad habits from developing in the first place. The most crucial aspect of preventing bad habits is to properly manage your puppy's environment. If you don't allow your dog to get into a situation where he might behave badly, he's unlikely to find out that he enjoys naughty activities.

Chewing is one of the biggest challenges that puppy owners will face. All puppies chew as they go through the various stages of teething, but Tibetan Mastiffs in particular are notorious for chewing. In order to prevent your furniture and precious belongings from being destroyed by your Tibetan Mastiff, you must manage his environment accordingly. This means keeping him away from opportunities to chew inappropriate items. You should never leave your Tibetan Mastiff unsupervised in your home, as doing so is just asking for trouble. This does not mean you should lock your puppy away while he's teething, but rather you should supervise him closely when he's in an area where he might chew furniture or belongings. By offering alternatives, such as edible chews and safe toys, you can provide him with an appropriate outlet for chewing. Until your Tibetan Mastiff understands what he is and is not allowed to chew, you will need to crate him or place him in a playpen or other secure area when you are unable to provide proper supervision.

Digging is another bad habit that is common with Tibetan Mastiff puppies. At first glance, digging may seem like it's more harmful to your landscaping than it is to your dog. However, dogs that dig often accidentally or purposefully ingest dirt, rocks, or sticks. They can also damage their nails and paw pads. The biggest risk with digging is that your dog may be able dig under your fence and escape. Like other bad habits, it's best to discourage this behavior before it gets out of hand. Richard Eichhorn of Drakyi Tibetan Mastiffs recommends burying your dog's droppings to discourage him from digging in that area. Do not leave your Tibetan Mastiff out in the yard unsupervised, especially for long periods of time. A bored or lonely Tibetan Mastiff is a destructive Tibetan Mastiff.

While supervising your dog's outings, if you see him begin to dig, clap your hands loudly to distract him and say "No!", similar to when you catch him relieving himself in the house. If your dog chooses to ignore you, you can reinforce your command by spritzing him with a spray bottle filled with water. The water will not harm your dog, but most dogs do not like being

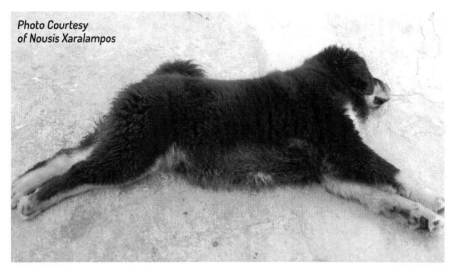

Photo Courtesy of Nousis Xaralampos

sprayed in the face so they learn to avoid these consequences by not repeating the offensive behavior. With enough consistent corrections, your dog will decide he has better things to do. Remember, inconsistent corrections will result in inconsistent behavior, so if you expect to discourage your dog from digging, you must do so every time you catch him in the act. You must also not allow him unsupervised access to the yard.

Another common problem with Tibetan Mastiffs is barking. Night barking, in particular, is common in guardian breeds and is simply a trait that has been bred into them over centuries of use as livestock and temple guardians. It's simply their way of announcing their presence to any potential intruders. Again, managing your dog's environment is the surest way to prevent this problem from developing. If you allow your dog unsupervised access to your yard during the night, he's likely to go straight to work guarding his property and his family and will warn potential intruders of his presence with his deep and powerful bark. Obviously, your neighbors won't appreciate how hard your dog works, so your best option is to keep your dog indoors. The same applies during the day. If you banish your dog to the backyard while you're at work, he's not only going to cause a ruckus, but he may develop other, more destructive bad habits due to his boredom and lack of mental stimulation. If you don't already have other pets, you may want to consider getting your Tibetan Mastiff a companion to keep him company while you're away and to discourage him from engaging in unwanted behavior.

Separation Anxiety

Although Tibetan Mastiffs may appear aloof and indifferent to strangers, they are fiercely loyal to their family and thrive on love and affection. As a result, they can develop separation anxiety if their environment and daily schedule is not managed appropriately. Tibetan Mastiffs are not a breed that can be turned loose on your property and ignored. Richard Eichhorn of Drakyi Tibetan Mastiffs says, "Social interaction is vital for proper psychological development. Lonely, bored, solitary dogs may become destructive or overly needy, with tendencies toward dog aggression and problem barking." Therefore, you'll need to provide your Tibetan Mastiff with plenty of attention, but in a way that leaves him with a healthy self-confidence in your absence.

Separation anxiety can be incredibly difficult to fix once the issue has arisen, so you must work hard to prevent your dog from developing this problem. The most crucial aspect in preventing separation anxiety is to not make a big deal about leaving or arriving at your home. Drawn out good-byes and overly enthusiastic hellos may feel nice in the moment, but they only serve to convince your dog that these are moments to be concerned about. Your dog will anticipate these moments and become stressed out. Instead, you need to convince him that he'll be fine regardless of whether you're home and that anytime you leave, you will most certainly be back soon. It can be difficult to leave for work without saying goodbye or telling your dog how much you missed him after a long day at the office, but you must remain calm and only acknowledge your dog once he has calmed down. The calmer you are in these situations, the calmer your dog will be.

Photo Courtesy of Nicole Moss

Dogs are pack animals and as such, they often do better with companions. If your Tibetan Mastiff is your only pet, you may want to consider adopting a companion for him. While many dogs prefer the company of their own kind, many will also do well with feline friends, but this will depend on your individual dog and his preferences.

If your Tibetan Mastiff seems stressed out in your absence or tends to destroy things while you're away, consider crating him while you're gone. Many dogs find comfort in their "den" and are more likely to behave themselves when crated. However, if you haven't taken the time to properly crate train your dog, the crate may just increase his stress. He may try to escape or destroy the crate, injuring himself in the process. In order for crating to be successful, you must take the time to properly introduce the concept to your dog, as discussed earlier. You must also provide him with enough physical and mental stimulation throughout the rest of his day that he will be willing to rest calmly when it's time to go in the crate.

Leaving Your Dog Home Alone

The first few times you leave your Tibetan Mastiff home alone can be stressful for you both, but with a little preparation it will go much more smoothly. The first step is making sure the area you're leaving your dog in is safe and secure. Whether you're leaving him in a crate, playpen, designated room, or safe outdoor area, you need to make sure that there is no way your dog can escape or hurt himself.

After ensuring that your Tibetan Mastiff will be safe in your absence, you can prepare him for being left home alone by leaving for just a few seconds at a time. Remember, don't make a big deal out of leaving or arriving. You can try leaving the house for just a few seconds at a time before returning. The more often you can leave and return without drama, the more comfortable your dog will be while you're gone. If your dog begins to act up or throw a tantrum, simply ignore him until he calms down. If you acknowledge him while he's upset, he'll only learn that his tantrums will get him attention. Ignoring this behavior will discourage him from acting up by teaching him that acting calmly will get him what he wants. Richard Eichhorn of Drakyi Tibetan Mastiffs also recommends distracting your Tibetan Mastiff with food, treats, or toys during this time.

Take It Slow

During the first few weeks with your new Tibetan Mastiff, your relationship will have its ups and downs. There will be times you are frustrated and times that you are overjoyed with your new family member. However, no matter what happens, you must be patient. This is a big change for everyone and even if things are difficult you must exercise patience at all times.

Although you'll want to start training your new companion right away, be sure to keep your training sessions short, light, and positive. Tibetan Mastiffs are unlikely to respond well to intense training sessions anyway, so try to keep sessions to just a few minutes at a time. Be sure to reward your Tibetan Mastiff generously when he responds to your commands and always end the session on a positive note. If you keep training your dog longer than he is comfortable with, you'll both become frustrated and less likely to enjoy future sessions. Above all, remember to enjoy your time with your new dog. This will be a long-term relationship, so you want to make sure you're setting off on the right foot.

Photo Courtesy of Nathaniel Askins

CHAPTER 8
Health and Wellness

Choosing a Veterinarian

If you do not have other pets in your household, it can seem like a daunting task to choose the right veterinarian for your new Tibetan Mastiff. However, with a little effort and research you can find a vet that will be able to work with you in keeping your new family member happy and healthy throughout his lifetime.

One of the best ways to find a good veterinarian is to ask your breeder or shelter for recommendations. Although shelters often have onsite veterinary care, many foster home-based rescues use specific vets that they have found to provide quality care, though often at a discount since they are non-profit organizations. Breeders, on the other hand, work closely with vets to provide both their adult dogs and new puppies with the best care possible. If your breeder is local, you'll have the benefit of working with a vet who knows the breed well and has known your puppy since his very first visit.

Unfortunately, if you've adopted your Tibetan Mastiff from a breeder or shelter some distance away from your home, you won't have the option to ask them for vet recommendations. Instead, try asking dog-loving friends and family who they would recommend. If you have acquaintances with large breeds,

NOT-SO-FUN FACTS
Health Problems

As large-breed dogs, Tibetan Mastiffs are prone to a variety of health problems, especially bone and joint problems. Some health problems your Tibetan Mastiff may be more prone to include:

- **Hip or Elbow Dysplasia** – a painful condition caused by a malformation of the joints

- **Osteochondrosis Dissecans (OCD)** – an improper growth of cartilage in the joints (usually the shoulder)

- **Entropion and Ectropion** – eyelids disorders that can require surgical correction

- **Panosteitis** – also known as "growing pains"

- **Hypothyroidism** – a deficiency of the thyroid hormone that causes many symptoms

Photo Courtesy of Tina De Boltz

their opinion can be especially valuable when searching for a vet for your new dog. You might also try attending local dog shows or breed club meetings and asking around.

When choosing a veterinarian, it's important to consider what type of clinic you're looking for. Most veterinary hospitals lean more toward traditional veterinary medicine, so if you're looking for a holistic vet or one that offers alternative treatments, you may to consult other resources. Both the American Veterinary Medical Association (AVMA) and the American Holistic Veterinary Medical Association (AHVMA), for example, offers directories of veterinarians on their website that you can search through. If you would prefer to take your Tibetan Mastiff in for regular care on Saturdays, rather than during the workweek, you'll need to find a clinic with weekend hours. Some clinics may also offer extended hours or may even be open around the clock. Veterinarians in higher income neighborhoods may charge more than those located in lower income areas. Some clinics may also offer low-cost vaccinations, spaying, and neutering at certain times of the month, so if you have budgetary limits, keep these options in mind when choosing a vet.

What to Expect During the First Visit

The most crucial part of your Tibetan Mastiff's first visit with a veterinarian will be his physical exam. During the exam, the vet will go over every inch of your dog to make sure he's as healthy as possible. This will involve weighing your dog to make sure he's at a healthy weight as well as a hands-on examination. Your veterinarian will run his or her hands along your dog's sides to confirm that his weight is appropriate for his frame. Tibetan Mastiffs have a lot of hair, so appearances can be deceiving unless you actually put your hands on the dog. The vet will also examine your new dog's teeth, ears, eyes, skin, and paws. His temperature, breathing, and heart rates will also be taken so that the vet can get a good overview of your dog's current health. Regardless of whether you brought home a puppy or an adult dog, it may be time for routine vaccines. If so, your veterinarian will discuss the course of action and will let you know what vaccinations must be performed at that time.

The first vet visit is also a great opportunity to make sure your new Tibetan Mastiff is free from parasites, both internal and external. Most exter-

nal parasites will be apparent in the physical exam, but internal parasites can be a bit more difficult to detect. Your veterinarian might want to perform a fecal exam in order to detect any intestinal parasites. By examining a sample of your dog's feces under a microscope, a veterinarian or veterinary technician will be able to detect the presence of adult worms, eggs, or protozoa, such as giardia. Even if there are no signs of infection, the veterinary team may suggest deworming your dog anyway just to be sure. If parasites are detected, the veterinarian will be able to identify the species of parasite so they can prescribe the correct treatment. Depending on the type of infection, treatment can range from a single oral dose to months of treatment. Roundworms, for example, are common in puppies and are easily treated, but heartworm infections require a lengthy treatment where the dog's activity levels must be severely limited. This is an excellent opportunity to discuss both flea and tick control and heartworm prevention so that you and your veterinarian can develop a long-term care plan for your Tibetan Mastiff.

If your new Tibetan Mastiff has not yet been spayed or neutered, you should consider discussing this with your veterinarian during the first visit. Even if your puppy is too young for the surgery, it's a good idea to develop a plan of action with your vet. Most vets recommend spaying or neutering at around six months of age, but your veterinarian will be able to give you a more accurate timeframe based on your dog's current health. Richard Eichhorn of Drakyi Tibetan Mastiffs recommends spaying females between 9 and 12 months of age. He suggests neutering males between 18 and 24 months of age to allow them to develop the size and secondary sex characteristics the breed is known for. If costs are a concern, it can also be helpful to get an idea of what you'll need to save to cover the cost of surgery. Some owners may also be stressed out about having their dogs undergo anesthesia, so if you have any questions or concerns, such as your breed's sensitivity to anesthesia, be sure to mention them to your vet.

Caring for Large Breeds

Although Tibetan Mastiffs are a relatively healthy breed, there are some health concerns that are common in large breed dogs. During your dog's first vet visit, you may consider discussing some of these problems with your veterinarian. Your vet will be able to assess your dog's risk level and develop a plan for the prevention or treatment of these issues.

Gastric Dilation Volvulus, also known as GDV or bloat, is a common condition in large breed dogs, though it can happen in smaller breeds as well. This medical emergency occurs when a dog's stomach fills with air. As the pressure builds, it can limit circulation and send the dog into shock. In more severe cases, the stomach can actually flip, cutting off blood flow to the stomach, spleen, and pancreas. Hormones are then released from the oxygen-starved pancreas, potentially causing the heart to stop. Even with treatment, bloat is fatal in about a third of all cases, regardless of severity.

Care must be taken by owners when feeding their large breed dogs to help reduce the risk of bloat. While some owners believe that elevated food bowls reduce the risk, this has not been proven. However, it has been proven that dogs that eat twice per day, rather than once, are less likely to bloat. Slow eaters are also at a lower risk of bloat than dogs who gulp, so if your Tibetan Mastiff eats quickly, you may need to use a different bowl to slow him down. It can also be helpful to reduce the stress of mealtime, so if you have multiple dogs you may need to separate them to reduce anxiety and gulping behavior. Dogs at risk for bloat may also undergo a preventative

Photo Courtesy of Amanda Armbruster

surgical procedure called a gastropexy, in which the stomach is tacked to the right side of the body wall to prevent twisting or flipping. Gases can still build within the stomach, but the procedure will help reduce the chances of fatality due to stomach torsion.

Joint and bone issues are also common in large breeds such as the Tibetan Mastiff. You should work with your veterinarian to ensure that your dog is receiving the right care to keep his joints as healthy as possible. Nutrition and weight can have a huge impact on the health of your dog's skeletal system, so be sure to discuss your dog's diet and weight to make sure he's getting the correct nutrients and not putting any unnecessary strain on his joints. If you've adopted an older dog, you may want to ask your veterinarian about adding join supplements to his diet to help prevent and ease the pain of arthritis.

Dangerous Foods

Many dog owners are aware of the danger of foods like chocolate, but there are a number of other human foods that can be potentially fatal if ingested by your dog. Foods containing caffeine or alcohol also present a danger to your dog, especially if ingested in large amounts. You must also be sure to keep your dog away from sugar-free gum and candy that may contain the artificial sweetener xylitol. Even in relatively small amounts, xylitol can be deadly. Onions, garlic, grapes, and raisins can also be toxic to dogs. If you suspect your Tibetan Mastiff may have eaten something toxic, call your local poison control or veterinarian immediately. The sooner you seek help, the better your dog's chances at survival.

There are also a few human foods that are not toxic to dogs, but should only fed in moderation, if at all. Foods that are high in fat, like peanut butter or cheese, should only be fed in small amounts. Excess fat consumption can put unnecessary stress on your dog's endocrine system. Overly salty foods, such as popcorn and ham, should also be avoided or fed only sparingly. Many adult dogs are also lactose-intolerant, so feeding your dog large amounts of milk, cottage cheese, or yogurt may result in gastrointestinal upset. Finally, foods that are high in sugar such as ice cream, cookies, or candy should also be avoided. Sugary desserts could upset your dog's stomach and the excess calories will only contribute to weight gain.

Common Health Problems in Puppies

Intestinal parasites are one of the most frequently encountered health problems in puppies of all breeds. Puppies become infected by consuming food, water, soil, or even another animal's feces, that has been contaminated with eggs or larvae. The most common types of worms found in puppies include roundworms, hookworms, tapeworms, and whipworms. However, protozoa such as giardia and coccidia are often found in puppies. Heartworms also pose a danger to puppies, but puppies do not typically show symptoms for several months after infection. Unlike intestinal parasites, heartworms are found in the heart and bloodstream.

Symptoms of internal parasites include vomiting, diarrhea, anemia, and weight loss. Puppies with a particularly heavy load of parasites may appear malnourished with a distended stomach. Lethargy and severe coughing are also possible. However, it should be noted that not all puppies will exhibit symptoms and even puppies that appear perfectly healthy could be infected. Your veterinarian will be able to perform the appropriate tests to determine whether your new puppy has any internal parasites and prescribe the proper treatment.

Fleas and ticks are also common in puppies and can be picked up from outdoor spaces, the mother dog, or other pets in the home. Severe itching and skin inflammation, also known as flea allergy dermatitis, is due to your dog's immune system reacting to the flea's saliva. In addition to extreme discomfort, fleas and ticks can also carry tapeworms, bartonellosis, Lyme disease, Rocky Mountain spotted fever, ehrlichiosis, and babesiosis. Anemia is also possible with heavy flea and tick infestations. Additionally, external parasites can be passed on to other pets or people in the home, so it's important to keep your puppy protected. As risk of disease varies according to location, your veterinarian will be able to suggest the right flea and tick prevention product for your area.

Gastrointestinal upset is also a problem that is frequently experienced by puppies. Many puppies are sensitive to sudden changes in their diet and may experience vomiting and diarrhea as a result. To minimize your puppy's tummy troubles if you plan on making dietary changes, you should do so slowly over a period of a few days or a week. A slow transition will give your Tibetan Mastiff's stomach a chance to adapt to the new food without causing upset. Treats should also be given in moderation and large chews should be taken away if your dog appears to be eating it quickly. It's also recommended to limit the amount of human food your dog gets. Human food is one of the most common reasons for gastrointestinal problems in puppies.

Due to a puppy's delicate immune system, contracting a serious illness is a very real possibility for any young dog. Until your Tibetan Mastiff puppy is fully vaccinated, typically at around 16 weeks of age, you should avoid public spaces as much as possible. You should also try to limit the number of strange people and animals in your home. You could be accidentally exposing your dog to dangerous viruses and bacteria. If you notice any severe symptoms such as anorexia, weight loss, fever, bloody diarrhea, incoordination, or weakness, you should seek veterinary care as soon as possible. Diseases such as parvovirus or distemper can be deadly if not treated immediately.

CHAPTER 9
Housetraining

"TMs are an alpha breed. If you don't train them, they are going to train you! Start young, with a short lesson each day. Keep it fun, and find a treat that motivates them."

Efrain Valle
Drakyi Tibetan Mastiffs

Photo Courtesy of Jade Brooks

Different Options for Housetraining

While there are a variety of housetraining tools and methods used by professional dog trainers, most owners of large breed dogs, such as Tibetan Mastiffs, opt for a more traditional approach to housetraining. This involves teaching a dog that the only appropriate place to relieve himself is outdoors and that he must alert you when he needs to go out. Some owners choose to teach their dogs to only use certain areas of their yard or outdoor space for their bathrooms needs. You may also rely on your dog to let you know when he needs to go out

HELPFUL TIP
Crate Training

Even if you don't plan on keeping your Tibetan Mastiff in a crate on a regular basis, it's a good idea to get him used to one while house-training him as a puppy. Your Tibetan Mastiff will probably encounter a kennel at some point in his life—like at the groomer or vet—and may be terrified to the point where he hurts himself if he wasn't acclimated to a crate as a puppy. Crates also act as your dog's safety belt while on long car rides, and many hotels will require your dog to be in a crate if left alone.

by pawing at the door, whining, barking, or pacing. You can hang bells, specifically designed for use with housetraining. To alert you to his need to go outside, your dog simply paws or nudges the bells.

Puppy pads and indoor potty patches are not practical for adult Tibetan Mastiffs, but they can help contain some of the mess while you're housetraining your puppy. Both options allow your dog to relieve himself in an appropriate area if you are unavailable to take him outside. While these options are rarely considered long-term options for large dogs, they can be incredibly helpful while your dog is learning the rules of the house and is unable to hold it for more than a few hours at a time.

Puppy pads may be either disposable or reusable. With disposable pads, you simply toss the plastic pads in the trash once they've been soiled and set out new pads as needed. Reusable pads are typically made of a waterproof fabric and can be laundered in a washing machine between uses. Potty patches are typically made of plastic and a type of fake grass or turf. They can be emptied and washed when necessary. It's not uncommon for owners to rely on indoor pads or patches for the first few weeks and transition to outdoor bathroom breaks as a puppy progresses in his training.

The First Few Weeks

During the early stages of housetraining your Tibetan Mastiff, you must practice patience and consistency. Accidents are inevitable, so you must be prepared to deal with them when they occur. When your dog has an accident, it's important not to punish him. Tibetan Mastiffs are highly sensitive and punishing your new dog may actually slow down your training rather than support it. If your Tibetan Mastiff has an accident and you do not catch him in the act, simply clean up the mess and move on. Never hit or spank your dog if he has an accident in the house. Rubbing his nose in his mess is inappropriate as well. None of these punishments will teach your dog not to relieve himself indoors. Instead, it will teach him to be fearful of you and he will then only go to the bathroom when you aren't around, probably in a hidden place.

If you catch your dog in the act of relieving himself in an inappropriate place, interrupt him with a loud clap or a sharp "No!" and immediately take him outside. Once outside, encourage him to continue by giving him a

command such as "Go potty!". When he's done, be sure to praise him with plenty of attention and treats. Supervision is incredibly important during the first few weeks of housetraining. The more consistently you catch your dog making a mistake, the more consistently you can provide corrections and guidance. If you allow your Tibetan Mastiff to roam your house unsupervised, you are allowing him to urinate and defecate wherever he pleases. And the more often he is allowed to do so, the slower your progress will be with housetraining.

Finding a mess can be frustrating, but don't take out that frustration on your new family member. This is where training aids may come in handy. The more you encourage your dog to make use of these products while under supervision, the more likely he is to use them instead of your living room rug if your attention lapses momentarily.

The Importance of Consistency

"TM's do not learn like other dogs. They are keenly intelligent and adhere to the things that are involved in guarding its fam¬ily and family belongings. Without guidance, a novice will get very frus¬trated and many times it results in lack of control/alpha manners. This leads to unhappy TM's and unhappy owners."

Debbie Parsons Slayton
Dreamcatcher Tibetan Mastiffs

Consistency is the single most important factor in housetraining success. If you aren't consistent in your Tibetan Mastiff's housetraining, his progress will be slow and frustrating. Housetraining requires a significant amount of effort and attention, from everyone in the family, so it's essential that all human family members are on board with your new dog's training program. Each family member should be aware of your puppy's bathroom schedule, supervision requirements, and what to do if you do or do not catch your new dog in the act of relieving himself indoors. Additionally, all capable members of the family should know where the cleaning supplies are located and how to thoroughly clean the area to discourage further marking.

Once your new companion, whether a puppy or an adult Tibetan Mastiff, begins to understand your expectations, you can begin relaxing your

Photo Courtesy
of Nousis Xaralampos

rules, but it's essential that you maintain a relatively rigid schedule at first. Puppies are not able to go for more than a few hours between bathroom breaks. This is also true for adults who have never been taught that they need to hold it for any period of time. Remember to take your dog outside after eating, napping, or playing. You'll need to be patient as your dog learns and gains the ability to go for longer periods between trips outside.

A good rule of thumb for puppies is that a puppy will be able to hold it for approximately one hour for every month of his age. For example, if your Tibetan Mastiff puppy is three months old, he should be able to wait a maximum of three hours before he needs to go. If you wait much longer, an accident is almost guaranteed. Unfortunately, this consistency needs to be in place around the clock, so be prepared for a few sleepless nights during your first few weeks at home with your new dog. As your new family member gains experience and understanding, you'll be able to predict when he'll need to go outside and can adapt your schedule accordingly.

Positive Reinforcement

One of the most widely used training methods, not just with housetraining, is positive reinforcement. This technique consists of rewarding your dog whenever he performs a desired behavior. In terms of housetraining, this means rewarding your Tibetan Mastiff every time he relieves himself in an appropriate area, such as your yard. With repetition, your dog will realize that when he performs the behavior, he receives praise or food, increasing the likelihood that he'll repeat it in the future. Tibetan Mastiffs tend to be independent thinkers, but most can be easily swayed with a tasty treat.

As with all aspects of housetraining, consistency is key. You need to build an association between going potty outside and the reward. This can be difficult if your puppy begins to associate going outside with playtime and exploration. In order to set clear boundaries for your new dog, you need to teach him that the reward of affection, treats, and playtime only comes after he's done his business.

When you first take your Tibetan Mastiff outside, he may be eager to run off and play, but you need to encourage him with the command "go potty" or something similar. Remain calm and quiet while you ask him to go to the bathroom, but be prepared to celebrate with him when he does finally relieve himself. You can encourage him with quiet praise during the act, but wait until he's done to tell him how good he is. If you interrupt him, he might lose focus. Once he's finished, you can lavish him with praise, pets, and playtime.

The specific type of reward you use with your Tibetan Mastiff will depend on his individual personality. If he's a food-driven dog, you may be able to reward him with treats or a small portion of his daily kibble. Picky dogs may not respond well to food-based rewards, however, so you may need to consider other options. Many Tibetan Mastiffs thrive on affection, so verbal praise and petting could work best. Although toys are not the most popular type of reward, some dogs respond best to playtime as a reward. Whether it's a game of tug, chase, or a lighthearted wrestling match, do whatever makes your Tibetan Mastiff happy. Remember, the more over-the-top the reward, the more likely it is that your dog will repeat the behavior in order to receive the same reward in the future.

Cleaning Up

During your Tibetan Mastiff's housetraining, messes are guaranteed to happen. No matter how consistent you are in your training and supervision, your dog will have an accident. Cleaning up the mess with the appropriate products and techniques will not only ensure that your house stays clean and sanitary, but it may even discourage your dog from returning to the same spot to mark.

When purchasing cleaning products, it's important to consider what type of floors you have in your home. Obviously, hard surfaces will be easier to clean than carpet, but you need to make sure you are choosing a product that will thoroughly clean and sanitize the surface. Feces can spread dangerous bacteria and even parasites, so it's crucial that you clean the area well. Urine can not only stain a surface but leave a lingering smell that will encourage your dog and others to return to that spot to mark their territory. Choose a cleaning product that is specifically designed for pet messes to reduce the chances that your Tibetan Mastiff will continue to use that area for his bathroom needs.

Carpet can be particularly tricky to clean, so you'll need to do what works best for the type of carpet in your home. With any cleaning product, it's best to test it in an area where any discoloration will not be noticed. Some carpet may begin to unravel with vigorous scrubbing or the use of brushes rather than towels, so use caution when cleaning pet messes. Richard Eichhorn of Drakyi Tibetan Mastiffs suggests covering the wet area after cleaning with a layer of table salt for a few days to help sanitize and dry

Photo Courtesy
of Fierariu Cornelia

the area. The salt can be vacuumed up afterwards. If you're struggling to remove stains or smells from your carpet, you may need to consult a carpet cleaning professional for advice or assistance.

In addition to a cleaning agent, you'll also need to stock up on items such as towels, paper towels, and scrub brushes. Paper towels are a great way to clean up and dispose of the mess, but they don't work well for scrubbing. Throughout the housetraining stage, you will go through a lot of paper towels. Small towels or cleaning cloths tend to be more durable and can be washed after use. If you have hard surfaces in your home, such as linoleum or tile, you might consider using a scrub brush to make sure you remove all residue. Some pet owners also find success with using household steam cleaners to sanitize their hard surface floors.

Playpens and Doggy Doors

As your Tibetan Mastiff progresses in his housetraining you may want to consider offering a bit more freedom. If you believe that he is ready, you can begin allowing him to stay in a playpen, rather than his crate, while you are away. A playpen will allow your puppy more space to move and play, but without the potential trouble that comes with access to the entire house. Even if you don't quite trust him enough to leave him in a playpen while you're away, it's a great option to give him a chance to stretch his legs while you're busy with household chores or are otherwise unable to properly supervise him. If you are concerned that he may have an accident, but trust him enough not to chew up puppy pads, consider lining the bottom of the playpen with either disposable or reusable pads.

If you'd like to give your Tibetan Mastiff even more freedom over his bathroom schedule, you might consider investing in a doggy door. Doggy doors let your dog choose when he goes outside, rather than waiting on you, which may mean fewer accidents in the house. There are several different types of doors available that can be temporarily installed in a sliding patio door or permanently installed in either a wooden door or wall. The doors come with varying levels of insulation to help prevent the loss of heat or cooling. Many doggy doors can also be locked, which is great if you don't want your dog going outside while you're at work or at night. If you have other pets that you don't want to go out or are worried about neighborhood strays or wildlife coming in, there are doggy doors that remain locked until they are approached with a "key" worn on your dog's collar. This special tag unlocks the door as your dog approaches but will relock as soon as he gets a certain distance away from the door.

Regardless of which type of doggy door you choose, it's important to make sure you choose the appropriate size. If you're buying a doggy door for a puppy, you'll either need to buy a size that he'll be able to fit through as an adult or purchase a bigger door when he outgrows the current one. If you choose the latter option, it may be best to invest in a temporary doggy door until you know what size your dog will need as an adult.

Whether you choose to give your Tibetan Mastiff a playpen or a doggy door, you must be certain that he's ready for that level of responsibility. Tibetan Mastiffs are clever dogs that are capable of getting into a lot of trouble if they don't receive enough mental and physical stimulation. More space or time outdoors is not an alternative to proper exercise and training sessions. It's also important that you make sure your dog's playpen or outdoor space is as secure as possible. Many types of playpens are not meant to withstand the weight of a Tibetan Mastiff and may be knocked over or climbed over rather easily. If your dog escapes his pen, he may cause trouble elsewhere in the house.

If you're using a doggy door, make sure there are no gaps in your fence or any other way that your dog could escape your yard. Tibetan Mastiffs like to wander and it's unlikely that your dog will stick around if he has the chance to explore the neighborhood. You'll also want to be cautious when leaving your dog home alone with access to the doggy door, as Tibetan Mastiffs are known for barking. It's common for guardian breeds to announce their presence with their powerful bark, but your neighbors might not appreciate how committed your dog is to his job. So, before you give your Tibetan Mastiff more freedom, consider whether he is truly ready for that or if he needs a bit more time and training.

CHAPTER 10
Socialization

"When introducing your TM to another new dog for the first time, introduce them off your property, if possible, on neutral territory."

Dan Smith
Sunset Tibetan

Photo Courtesy
of Jade Brooks

The Importance of Good Socialization

One of the greatest benefits of properly socializing your Tibetan Mastiff is that you'll be able to take him anywhere. Good socialization will give your dog the confidence and skills to handle new situations, no matter what you may encounter. This will enable you to take your dog with you wherever you like. Whether you're going to a highly competitive dog show in another state or to lunch at the local café, you'll be

HELPFUL TIP
Socialization Prevents Aggression

Tibetan Mastiffs have been bred for thousands of years to be impressive guard dogs. They need to learn from an early age that most other people and animals are "safe." Without proper socialization, your Tibetan could become very territorial toward strangers and other animals.

able to take your Tibetan Mastiff knowing that he will be a welcome guest at any dog-friendly establishment. Remember, Tibetan Mastiffs are a naturally suspicious breed, so you're going to need to work on socialization regularly throughout your dog's life.

Most importantly, good socialization is essential to your Tibetan Mastiff's overall happiness and wellbeing. Tibetan Mastiffs are incredibly loving dogs that are devoted to their families. The more time they spend with their people, the happier and more well-adjusted they are. A properly socialized dog will be able to make more friends and have more opportunities to play. Not only is this beneficial to your dog's mental health, but the physical activity will keep him fit and happy. Remember, a well-exercised Tibetan Mastiff is less likely to be destructive.

Without proper socialization, Tibetan Mastiffs can become fearful, aggressive, and difficult to manage. Your dog could become a liability if he believes that he needs to protect his home from someone that he deems as a threat. Socialization will result in a more stable, confident companion that you can trust. Even if you don't plan on showing or traveling with your Tibetan Mastiff, he'll still need to be seen regularly by a vet or groomer. If he is exposed to these types of situations early on, your dog is more likely to handle himself in public with the calm confidence that the breed is known for.

Socializing Puppies

Ideally, your puppy's breeder will have started socializing him before you take him home. Most reputable breeders believe in starting the socialization process as early as possible. According to Richard Eichhorn of Drakyi Tibetan Mastiffs, "Early interaction with humans is essential and helps the pups adjust more quickly to their new homes." However, there is a limit on how much an unvaccinated or under-vaccinated puppy should be exposed to, so you'll need to continue the process as your puppy grows and progresses through his vaccination schedule.

There are plenty of experiences that you can expose your Tibetan Mastiff to without risking his health. While you may not be able to immediately take him to experience the sights and sounds of a local obedience competition, you can certainly get him used to the sensation of being groomed. The more you can get your puppy used to being handled, the easier it will be for him to be handled by professionals such as veterinarians and groomers. Remember, socialization is best done in steps, so consider these early stages to be the foundation of your puppy's socialization. The more comfortable he is being handled at home, the less likely he is to panic the first time he experiences it in a clinic or grooming salon.

Photo Courtesy of R. Eichhorn & E. Valle

Drakyi Emperor Trajan, 4 months

As soon as your Tibetan Mastiff puppy is completely vaccinated, you should begin exposing him to as many people, animals, and situations as possible. Deborah Mayer of Noble Legacy Tibetan Mastiffs suggests, "If you have frequent guests, then make sure your pup is exposed to strangers in the home early on. If you like to take road trips, take your pup in the car with you wherever you go and get your

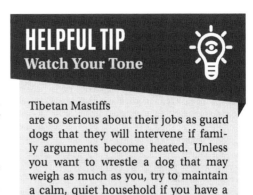

HELPFUL TIP
Watch Your Tone

Tibetan Mastiffs are so serious about their jobs as guard dogs that they will intervene if family arguments become heated. Unless you want to wrestle a dog that may weigh as much as you, try to maintain a calm, quiet household if you have a Tibetan Mastiff.

pup on the road as soon as their vaccination sequence is completed. If you plan to show your pup, sign up for handling classes or puppy matches in your area. Do it young and do it often."

It's important to note that although you should expose your puppy to as many unique experiences as possible, you should be careful not to overwhelm him. Early socialization will only be successful if the experiences are positive. If your puppy begins to show signs of fear or anxiety, it may be time to back off and try again at another time. While places like the local dog park may seem like a great place to socialize a playful puppy, the chaotic atmosphere can be overwhelming and can leave a negative impression. As your Tibetan Mastiff's caretaker, it's your job to set him up for success and part of that job involves managing his environment in a way that allows him to experience the world in a positive light.

Socializing Adult Dogs

If you've decided to adopt an adult Tibetan Mastiff, you should be aware that socializing adult dogs can be somewhat difficult compared to puppies. With puppies, every experience is new so you can expect them to be a little timid or unsure of themselves. With adult dogs, it can be difficult to know how much experience the dog has in certain situations and his reactions may be unpredictable at times. Even if the shelter or breeder claimed that your new family member is already well-socialized, you should still be prepared to encounter situations in which your dog may be uncomfortable.

As with puppies, you need to manage your Tibetan Mastiff's socialization in a way that only sets him up for success. If you know your dog doesn't do well with strangers, you shouldn't take him to a busy public park where he's likely to be approached by dozens of new people. Instead, you need to take things slowly. Socialization does involve taking your dog out of his comfort zone, but it must be done in a way that leaves a positive impression on him. Start by introducing him to one new person or take him to a quiet park where he can observe people from afar but won't be mobbed by them. Let him observe new experiences from a distance and approach only when he is comfortable.

Patience and understanding are crucial when it comes to socializing adult dogs. Your Tibetan Mastiff may have had negative experiences in his past that you will need to overcome. It's possible to overcome many past traumas, but it will take time and repetition. If your dog had a bad experience with another dog in a previous home, you won't be able to introduce him to one new friend and expect him to get along with every new dog he meets. Repeated attempts will be necessary, and you will need to monitor your dog closely to ensure that the encounter goes as planned. It may take weeks, months, or even years to overcome significant traumas, so you must remain patient and committed to your dog's socialization.

Photo Courtesy of Richard Eichhorn & Efrain Valle Drakyi Tibetan Mastiffs

L to R, Potala, Venus, Leona, Leo. Front, Phoenix

Lifelong Socialization

Socialization is not a process that can be completed during puppyhood. It is a lifelong activity that must be done regularly no matter your dog's age. Throughout your dog's life, he will continue to learn, grow, and develop. Even dogs who were well-socialized as puppies can develop behavioral problems due to bad experiences, so you must continue to guide your dog through difficult or uncomfortable circumstances. As you work with him through these unpleasant situations, not only will he become more confident in himself, but he'll become more confident in your ability to take care of him. With repetition, he'll come to trust that you'll never put him in a situation that is dangerous or overwhelming. Through socialization, you'll also strengthen the bond between you and your Tibetan Mastiff.

One of the greatest benefits of lifelong socialization is the mental and physical stimulation provided by the exposure to new experiences. Whether it involves taking your Tibetan Mastiff hiking or on a playdate at a friend's house, you can rest assured that your Tibetan Mastiff will benefit from the experience. The benefits of ongoing socialization are innumerable. Not only will he enjoy spending time with you away from the house, but the mental and physical exercise he receives will help him be calmer and better behaved in your home.

Lifelong socialization is especially important to Tibetan Mastiffs due to their tendency to be suspicious of strangers and new situations. As a guardian breed, Tibetan Mastiffs are inclined to protect their family and property from potential threats. As your new companion continues to grow and develop, it's essential that you socialize him in a way that teaches him that he doesn't need to be on duty all the time. As this trait is ingrained in the breed, it's something that you'll need to work on continuously.

Dealing with Fear

During the socialization process, you will encounter situations in which your Tibetan Mastiff will show fear. The only way to prevent your dog from becoming afraid is to never expose him to anything that may scare him. Unfortunately, this is not an option. The essential part of this experience is how you deal with your dog's fear.

Keeping a close eye on your Tibetan Mastiff's body language is essential in monitoring and controlling his fear. Mild signs of fear or anxiety include trembling, hiding, tucking the tail under the body, and avoidance. Your dog

Photo Courtesy
of Nikki Love

may also flatten his ears, cower, lick his lips, or yawn. Dogs that display mild signs such as these can usually be calmed down or kept under control. However, if your dog begins to panic you may see increased panting and pacing, or he may actively try to escape you. In those cases, you need to get him out of the situation or back off a bit. It's common for dogs to react aggressively out of fear if they feel they have no other option, so you need to take your dog's warning signs seriously.

If your Tibetan Mastiff does begin to show fear or anxiety while socializing him, it's important that you react appropriately. Do not try to comfort or soothe your dog during this time as it may be misinterpreted as encouragement. You may feel as though you're alleviating your dog's discomfort, but he will interpret it as confirmation that he has something to worry about. Instead, you need to set an example for your dog. Remain calm and confident no matter what happens. By minimizing your reactions, you're letting your dog know that there is nothing to worry about.

If you've gotten your Tibetan Mastiff into a situation during his socialization that did not go as planned, back off and examine the situation after the fact. Consider what went wrong and what you could have done differently. Socialization and training are a learning opportunity for you too, so take advantage of your mistakes and learn from them. If you are struggling to figure out what could have been done differently or you can't seem to overcome a certain problem, consider reaching out to a professional. Canine behaviorists and professional trainers may have the answer you're looking for. It's especially important to work with a professional if you're working with a dog with extreme fearfulness. It can be easy to further traumatize a dog with fear issues and it's best to work with someone experienced in dealing with this type of behavioral problem.

If you do encounter a situation where your Tibetan Mastiff reacts with extreme or unexpected fear, it's essential that you realize it will take time for your dog to overcome these obstacles in his socialization. Behavioral problems do not develop overnight and they are not resolved overnight either. As with other aspects of your dog's training, it's essential that you stay consistent and committed to your Tibetan Mastiff's socialization. There may be bumps in the road along the way, but as long as you stay dedicated to your dog's training and reach out to professionals when necessary, you'll be able to reach your goals of having a well-socialized Tibetan Mastiff.

Photo Courtesy of Dani Allen Smith

CHAPTER 11
The Multi-Pet Household

"Having had TMs for many years, both showing and breeding, my dogs had to live in peaceful harmony. The show world is tricky for any TMs that do not get along at home. The travel, show ring, and hotel rooms are a must, so if you decide to do these fun outings, make sure your TMs are ALL good together!"

Nancy Young
Hoshen Tibetan Mastiffs

Introducing a Puppy to Other Animals

Introducing your Tibetan Mastiff puppy to the other pets in your home is an essential step in developing their lifelong relationship. When introducing a puppy to your other animals, you typically need to worry more about the other animals not reacting well to the puppy than the other way around. Puppies are inexperienced enough in the world that even if they do show nervousness or fear toward other animals in the beginning, it's relatively easy to calm them down and get them through it.

When introducing your Tibetan Mastiff puppy to your other animals, whether they are household pets or livestock, it's important to restrain both animals for their protection. Keeping your puppy on a harness or collar and leash will allow you to remove him from the situation if you need to. With animals that don't do well on leashes, such as poultry or livestock, keeping them on the other side of a fence is best. The barrier will allow your puppy to approach the animals while making sure that no one gets hurt.

Go slowly and allow each animal to observe each other from a distance before moving them closer. Your puppy may be either curious or fearful toward the other animal, and vice versa, but it's important to allow everyone enough space to calm down. Once the animals seem comfortable, you can allow them to move closer and even sniff each other. Certain animals may not be interested in your puppy and that's fine as long as there is no fear, aggression, or anxiety. If either animal begins to panic, separate them immediately. You can always try again later.

Even if your Tibetan Mastiff is destined for life as a part-time livestock guardian, he may not be comfortable with his flock or herd at first, so only move as slowly as he is comfortable with. The more frequently you allow the animals to interact, the more quickly they'll get along so don't be afraid to try introductions several times per day. Eventually, the animals will either actively get along or show no interest in each other.

During the first few weeks or months, it's essential that you never allow the animals to inter-

HELPFUL TIP

Introducing Your Tibetan Mastiff to Other Pets

Since Tibetan Mastiffs were bred to be guard dogs, they can be wary of other animals. However, once they understand that other pets are part of the household they are meant to protect, they should be fine. The key is to see how your other pets react to such a large dog joining them in your home.

act without supervision. Although guarding is a natural instinct with this breed, you never know how a dog is going to react to an animal that he has no experience with. Only when you are certain that everyone's safety is guaranteed can you allow your Tibetan Mastiff to interact with your other animals without supervision.

Although some Tibetan Mastiffs have a higher prey drive than others, most will be able to get along well with any type of animal as long as they are introduced at a young age. There will be some dogs, however, that will require supervision or separation from certain types of animals throughout their life. Use caution when introducing your puppy to small pets such as rabbits, chickens, or cats. If your puppy continues to show aggressive behavior toward these animals, you may need to keep them separated. Remember, dogs are predators, and many have a strong natural instinct to hunt smaller animals, especially when they run from the dog. With training, your dog can learn to better control his impulses, but he may never be allowed unsupervised interactions with certain animals.

Photo Courtesy
of Bonni Bailey

Introducing an Adult Dog to Other Animals

Due to an adult dog's past experiences, it can often be more challenging to introduce them to other animals. An adult Tibetan Mastiff may have little to no experience with small pets or livestock or he may have had negative experiences in the past. Unless your new Tibetan Mastiff had only one home prior to yours, it can be difficult to know for sure what kinds of animals he has been introduced to. For the safety of both your Tibetan Mastiff and the other animals, it's best to behave as though you're introducing them for the first time and exhibit the appropriate level of caution.

As with puppies, you'll want to make sure that all animals are properly restrained. An adult Tibetan Mastiff can quickly and easily harm another animal, even if it's significantly bigger. Likewise, it doesn't take much of a kick from a horse or cow to injure a dog, so it's best to keep everyone restrained if possible. If things go badly, you want to be able to separate the animals as quickly as possible. Once all animals are properly restrained, you can go about the introductions the same way as you would with puppies.

Since adult dogs often have behavioral issues to deal with, you may need to be more patient when introducing your Tibetan Mastiff to other animals. Go as slowly as you need to in order to ensure everyone's safety and comfort. If you are struggling with your Tibetan Mastiff's behavior around other animals, whether it be fear or aggression, you may need to consult a professional trainer or canine behaviorist. If you feel that you cannot handle your dog's reactions, or are simply unsure of how to handle them, seek professional help as soon as possible. The sooner you reach out the sooner the problem can be solved. It's always best to start working on behavioral problems before they have the chance to escalate.

Fighting and Bad Behavior

"They have an interesting social structure. Males are ultimately dominant and will be the General, but the oldest dominant female will run the day to day operations. It is important that this female be fairly even tempered because she will kind of keep order among the younger females if you add more. There will be squabbles and in general it is better to let the older female settle these because bites are VERY common when trying to break up fights."

Dr. Charles Radcliffe
Timberline Tibetan Mastiffs

If your Tibetan Mastiff begins to show even the slightest signs of aggression, you need to act immediately. It may start out as a simple growl or pushing your other dog away from the food bowl, but if there are no consequences to your dog's aggression, it can quickly escalate into more serious and dangerous behavior. This is especially true if the other dog is significantly smaller than your Tibetan Mastiff. Fights can result in serious and even life-threatening injuries, so you need to correct aggressive behavior at the start. Do not allow your Tibetan Mastiff to bully your other pets or display resource guarding behavior. This does not mean your dogs are not allowed to have their own personal boundaries, but these boundaries should be reasonable. Discourage your dog's aggressive behavior by responding

Photo Courtesy
of Nikki Love

with a loud clap, stomp, or "No!" You can also redirect your Tibetan Mastiff's attention by calling him away from the situation or asking him to perform basic commands such as sit or down. If you can distract him from whatever inspired the aggressive behavior, you can diffuse the situation.

While working on your Tibetan Mastiff's aggressive behavior, it's crucial that you determine what is causing the aggression. You can provide as many corrections as you need, but if you don't know the underlying cause for the behavior, you'll never be able to completely eradicate it. Each time you catch your dog in an act of aggression, consider what these incidents have in common. If your dogs are constantly fighting over chew toys, you may need to either remove the toys from your home or only allow the dogs to enjoy them while separated. If your Tibetan Mastiff is displaying resource guarding behavior, you may need to work with him on learning how to share. Without knowing what is causing your dog's aggression, you'll never be able to completely solve the problem.

If your Tibetan Mastiff's aggression does escalate into an actual fight, it's essential that you understand how to safely intervene. Never break up a fight by grabbing one or both dogs. The dogs may be so focused on the fight that they don't pay attention to what it is that they're biting and you can become seriously injured in the process. Depending on the severity of the fight, whether it's a scuffle or an all-out brawl, there are a few different options you can try. For minor scuffles, a loud noise may be enough to stop the fight. This is the only time that it is appropriate to yell at your dogs. You can also try stomping, clapping, or banging on your dog's metal dishes. If that doesn't work, you can also try throwing water on the dogs or spraying them with a hose or spray bottle. The water won't hurt the dogs, but it often surprises them enough to stop them from fighting. You can also try tossing a blanket or sheet on top of them. If you absolutely must physically intervene, first decide which dog is the aggressor in the fight and which dog is defending himself. Grab the more aggressive dog by the hind legs and quickly pull him away from the other dog. You need to do this quickly to prevent the dog from turning around and biting you. Once the dogs have been pulled apart, restrain them or separate them as quickly as possible to prevent them from returning to the fight.

Aggression and fighting are serious and difficult behaviors to manage. They are dangerous not only to your other pets but your human family members as well. It's crucial that you recognize when you are no longer able to control your dogs' behavior and seek help immediately. The sooner you can contact a professional trainer or behaviorist, the less likely it is that the behavior will escalate. Dog fights should be taken seriously so if you're dealing with this problem, seek help as soon as possible.

Raising Multiple Puppies from the Same Litter

"Several people have had success keeping multiple males together, but this is only possible if there are NO females in the household. I would only recommend this to very experienced dog people and anytime you try multiple males in any arrangement you must be prepared with space, fences and shelters to keep them separate permanently if things don't work out."

Dr. Charles Radcliffe
Timberline Tibetan Mastiffs

Bringing home littermates can seem like a great idea at first, especially if you have no other animals at home. Two Tibetan Mastiffs that have been together since birth will be more confident coming into your home since they're already with a familiar companion. You'll never have to worry about your dog being home alone or introducing an unfamiliar dog. You will also have to put less effort into keeping your dogs busy since they'll always have a playmate, even if you're busy with work or household chores.

However, it's important to note that there are numerous drawbacks to having multiple puppies from the same litter. More puppies mean more trouble and more work for you. You'll need to spend more time supervising and training, so you'll need to manage your time wisely. Adopting dogs that have already formed a bond is great when you can leave them together, but if you ever need to take one away, to the vet for example, they may both react with stress and anxiety. Dogs who have never been alone can be extremely insecure and fearful without their companion and may act out in destructive ways. Housetraining can also be difficult when you have multiple puppies to monitor and take outside. Additionally, if your dogs are allowed to develop bad habits, it can be incredibly difficult to break multiple dogs of their bad behavior.

Adopting two or more puppies from the same litter has its pros and cons, which you need to consider carefully before committing. If you work full-time and have any hobbies, you may find that raising a single puppy is difficult enough. If you do decide to bring home multiple puppies, consider taking each out on their own on a regular basis to prevent separation anxiety and allow them to develop their own individual sense of confidence. It's also important that you regularly train them together as you may find yourself in a situation where you need to have all the puppies under con-

*Photo Courtesy
of Carol Czerw*

trol at once, which may be difficult if you've only ever worked with them individually.

If you're unsure of whether you can manage multiple puppies, but don't want your Tibetan Mastiff to be alone, consider adopting one dog first and once he's been properly trained and socialized, you can adopt a companion for him. This way, your dog will only be alone for a few months, but it will give you enough time to teach your first dog to be a responsible member of the family before shifting your focus to the next.

Options If Your Pets Don't Get Along

When introducing your Tibetan Mastiff to your existing pets, it's important to realize that they may not get along right away. Some pets may simply need more time to adjust to their new companion. This is especially true with older pets or those that have been alone for a long time. Don't rush the introductions and don't try to force the animals to get along any sooner than they're ready. It can take weeks, or even months, before your pets begin to get along. Patience is key, but you must also be willing to commit a significant amount of time to working with your pets and familiarizing them with each other. You might also want to consider seeking the advice of a professional trainer or behaviorist if you're struggling with your pets' relationship.

Photo Courtesy
of Dr. Charles Radcliffe
Timberline Tibetan Mastiffs

If you've exhausted your options and the thought of giving up one of your beloved pets is not an option you're willing to consider, then you'll need to develop a plan to keep them separated. It will take a lot of time and effort to keep your pets separate for their entire lives. You'll also need to ensure that each of them is receiving the same amount of care, exercise, and affection. You will need to make sure that each pet has a safe and adequately sized space to retreat to while staying out of reach from the other. Managing this type of lifestyle can be exhausting, stressful, and time-consuming, so you need to carefully consider whether you are truly willing or able to provide this level of care for them.

If you've decided that you are unwilling or unable to manage your pets' behavior any longer and keeping them separated isn't an option, you need to consider finding a more appropriate home for one of them. Some pets just prefer a single-pet home, while others may just need a different environment in order to thrive. As heartbreaking as it may be, it's your responsibility as your pets' caretaker to make the right decisions regarding their wellbeing.

CHAPTER 12
Training your Tibetan Mastiff

"Training a Tibetan Mastiff is dependent on how well you can pull it away from its guarding duties. Because the dog wants to please you, there is an understanding you can reach with your Tibetan Mastiff that, for a brief training moment, it will allow you to be a distraction."

Carol Gordon
Kachar Village Tibetan Mastiffs

Training and Puppy Classes

Informal training and socialization should begin the moment you bring your new Tibetan Mastiff home. While you don't need to start teaching your dog actual commands as soon as you walk in the door, you should begin to establish the rules of your household immediately. It can be tempting to be lenient with your dog the first few days, but the sooner you intro-

Photo Courtesy of R. Eichhorn and E. Valle

CH Drakyi Resurrection

duce the rules, the more easily he will adapt. You don't have to be strict, but you must be consistent. Remember, Tibetan Mastiffs are not enthusiastic about formal training, but they are perfectly capable of learning how to properly behave in a home. Consistency in your training will be the only way to convince your Tibetan Mastiff to listen to you.

HELPFUL TIP
Not for Dog Sports

While most dogs thrive on the physical and mental stimulation of performing in dog sports like agility, obedience, or flyball, Tibetan Mastiffs are too stubborn and disinterested to excel at dog sports. Your Tibetan may or may not decide to obey you at any given moment.

Once your Tibetan Mastiff has been fully vaccinated, you can begin his formal education by enrolling him in a puppy class. Most puppy classes will require your dog to be of a certain age before he's allowed to attend. They will also require proof of your puppy's vaccinations. Some training facilities may also require proof of treatment for fleas and ticks. This requirement is intended to protect your puppy as well as the others in the class. Parasites and disease can spread quickly among puppies with delicate immune systems, so it's best to make sure your puppy is protected before exposing him to potential illnesses.

Depending on the area you live in, you may have quite a few options for puppy classes. Such classes may be held at formal obedience schools, shelters, pet stores, and community centers. Feel free to check out a few different options before making your choice. Your breeder or shelter may also be able to recommend a specific trainer or facility that they've worked with in the past. Many shelters and rescue organizations offer low-cost training classes as part of their contribution to the community. If you'd prefer not to take your Tibetan Mastiff out for training, you can also have a professional trainer work with you in your home. This can be especially helpful with nervous dogs or those with behavioral problems.

If you've adopted an adult Tibetan Mastiff, your dog will not be allowed in puppy classes, but the same facilities or individuals that offer puppy classes will likely have basic obedience classes for adult dogs as well. As with puppy classes, your dog will need to be fully vaccinated before he's allowed to attend. Before you commit to an obedience class, consider whether it is the right option for you and your Tibetan Mastiff. For under-socialized, nervous, or aggressive dogs, group classes can be overwhelming. If you're unsure of whether group classes or individual sessions are right for you, speak to the trainer before signing up to explain your situation. They'll be able to recommend the right course of action for you and your Tibetan Mastiff.

Obedience classes for dogs of any age are a great opportunity for socialization. Instead of the chaotic environment of the dog park, obedience classes offer your dog a way to socialize in a safe and controlled environment. Socialization is especially important with Tibetan Mastiffs, so you want to do what you can to set your dog up for success. Proper socialization will leave a positive impression on your dog and will help discourage him from becoming fearful or aggressive with new people and dogs in the future. It's also an excellent way to get your dog used to traveling in the car and going new places. Remember, a well socialized dog will be a calmer and more confident companion, no matter where life takes you.

Photo Courtesy of Maria Folkomina

Benefits of Proper Training

"They like consistency and to know their PERSON is in charge. If they sense they are the leader - things get out of hand."

Judy Nowland
Tibetan Mastiffs of Alaska

Regular training sessions with your Tibetan Mastiff are a great way to prevent boredom and keep his mind and body exercised. Sessions that are as short as five to ten minutes each will not only strengthen the bond between you and your dog, but they provide your dog with an opportunity to exercise his mind and body. Training sessions tend to wear dogs out much faster than physical activity alone, so the sessions don't have to be long. A Tibetan Mastiff who regularly receives mental and physical stimulation will be calmer and more well-behaved in your home. A calm dog will also be more focused on what you're asking in the next training session.

It is important to note that even the most well-trained Tibetan Mastiff may not be able to safely accompany you to work or to run errands. If your goals are to simply take a daily stroll around the neighborhood, proper training will give your dog the skills necessary to make your daily walks something that you look forward to rather than dread. However, Tibetan Mastiffs are a territorial guardian breed that would generally prefer to stay home and guard their property than go with your family on vacation.

Richard Eichhorn of Drakyi Tibetan Mastiff emphasizes the challenge of training this breed with his experience in China:

"On a judging trip to Anyang, China in 2007, I was invited to a military dog training facility to observe their work with Tibetan Mastiffs. Skeptical, I accepted and met the director of the facility, a commanding officer who had worked with German Shepherds for 25 years.

From an observation room, we all watched as ten young military men lined up in the field, each with the Tibetan Mastiff they had been training since the dogs were puppies. They then each proceeded to put their dogs through their paces, performing various tricks, jumps and routines on command, individually, and as a group. I was conflicted seeing this, fearing that the independent spirit of the dogs had been broken, but the dogs were very bonded to their handlers, and wanted to perform.

I spoke with the director and asked about the training process. He said that the Tibetan Mastiffs required four times the work, time, and training to get the same behavior as a German Shepherd due to their independent nature. The individual dogs had to be carefully selected from their litters of origin as the breed is not best suited for repetitive training behavior.

Although your Tibetan Mastiff is unlikely to become a star in the obedience ring, if you plan on showing him in any other sport, you'll find that some basic obedience training will help you to achieve your competition goals. Additionally, basic training will help make socialization easier. Overall, proper training is crucial in raising a happy, well-rounded Tibetan Mastiff.

Operant Conditioning Basics

Originally studied and promoted by psychologist and behaviorist B.F. Skinner, operant conditioning is one of the most common learning methods employed by dog trainers. Skinner originally developed his theory based on his belief that humans and animals are much too complex to learn through classical conditioning alone. He believed that if certain behaviors were followed by positive experiences, the learner was more likely to repeat the behavior. Conversely, if the behavior was followed by a negative experience, the learner would be discouraged from repeating the behavior in the future.

In his studies, Skinner identified three environmental responses that shape behavior: neutral operants, reinforcers, and punishments. Neutral operants occur when a certain behavior is followed by an environmental response that neither increases nor decreases the likelihood of the behavior being repeated. For instance, if you responded to your dog's behavior by calmly explaining in detail what he did correctly, your dog will not understand you and your response will likely have no effect on his future behavior. Reinforcers can be either positive or negative and increase the probability of the behavior being performed in the future. Examples of reinforcers include treats, affection, or play. Punishments serve to discourage the learner from repeating the behavior. Punishments can be merely unpleasant, such as loud noises, or painful, but painful punishments should be avoided in training at all costs.

Operant conditioning is most frequently used in dog training in the form of positive reinforcement. Positive reinforcement is one of the most popular and effective training methods as most dogs are highly motivated by either food or praise. Once a dog performs a desired behavior, the trainer responds with either treats or affection, encouraging the dog to re-

Photo Courtesy
of Nousis Xaralampos

peat the behavior in the future, usually on command. Unfortunately, positive reinforcement also works in the development of bad behaviors. If your Tibetan Mastiff bolts out the open front door and is rewarded with an off-leash romp around the neighborhood, he's likely to repeat that behavior in the future. This is why you must be careful about managing your dog's behavior and environment. Bad habits can develop quickly if you aren't paying attention.

Negative reinforcement is also used in dog training, though less frequently than positive reinforcement. This training method tends to get a bad rap due to the confusion between negative reinforcement and punishment. In fact, many trainers employ this method without even realizing it. Negative reinforcement encourages the repetition of a desired behavior by removing an unpleasant stimulus from the dog's environment. For instance, when you're leash training your Tibetan Mastiff, you want to teach him to give in to the pressure of the leash. To accomplish this, you may put a small amount of pressure on the leash to encourage him to follow you. This is the unpleasant stimulus. If he tries to back up or move away, the pressure continues. When your dog takes a step in the right direction, the pressure is removed immediately. Soon, the dog will understand that if he gives into the pressure instead of fighting it, he can make the pressure go away.

Punishments can be differentiated from negative reinforcement because they are negative experiences that discourage certain behaviors from being repeated in the future. For example, if your Tibetan Mastiff tries to chew on your sofa and his actions are met with a loud clap, stomp, or "No!", he will likely view this unpleasant sound as a punishment. If this happens every time he tries to eat the sofa, he'll eventually learn that this behavior will be met with loud, awful noises which will discourage him from repeating the behavior in the future.

It's important to note that punishments should never be harsh. Hitting, kicking, or screaming at your dog will not teach him anything. Instead, you'll end up with a fearful or aggressive dog. Typically, punishments consist of claps, stomps, yelp, or a spray of water. They are not meant to cause your dog any pain, but instead are intended to distract him from his inappropriate behavior.

*Photo Courtesy
of Nicole Moss*

Essential Commands

"Some TMs will make eye contact with you immediately and let you know they are there to please you and learn. If the dog doesn't do that: work on it. Have treats ready and teach him 'Watch me'. He should bring his eye to you, then quickly reward. Once the dog will do that-you are set."

Judy Nowland
Tibetan Mastiffs of Alaska

Although there is technically no limit to what you can teach your Tibetan Mastiff, the basic commands discussed in this section are crucial to any dog's education. Regardless of whether you're raising a future champion or a companion, your Tibetan Mastiff will need to know essential skills such as name recognition, sit, and down. In order to uphold the rules of the house, your new dog will also need to know how to get off the furniture or give up a toy when you ask. Walking politely on a leash is also an important skill for any dog to learn. Remember, Tibetan Mastiffs can be a challenge to train, so try to focus on one or two commands at a time to prevent any confusion. This breed does not respond well to repetition, so keep your training sessions short and provide plenty of positive reinforcements. You may find that some days your Tibetan Mastiff would rather patrol his property than listen to your commands, so it's important to keep your training expectations low.

Name Recognition

Teaching your dog to recognize his name should begin the moment you bring your Tibetan Mastiff home. If your new family member has already been given a name, he may already recognize it. This skill must be taught to your dog before you can move on to more advanced commands as it's the basis for grabbing your dog's attention.

To teach your Tibetan Mastiff to respond to his new name, start with a handful of his favorite treats or kibble. Begin by saying his name and immediately handing him a treat. At first, he won't understand the connection but will gladly gobble up the treats. Sessions don't need to be long, even a minute or two is plenty at first. Repeat these sessions several times per day until your dog begins to pay attention to you every time you say his name. With practice, he'll begin to understand that when you say his name, you want his attention and there may be something delicious waiting for him when he listens.

Sit

The sit command is typically one of the first commands taught to dogs because it's a simple task that most puppies and adults can pick up relatively quickly. However, it's important to remember that it may take a lot of work to get your Tibetan Mastiff to perform this task on command. Short, frequent training sessions are key. It also puts your Tibetan Mastiff in a position where he can better see your face and anticipate what your next moves are. The sit command is especially useful in teaching your dog household manners like waiting politely for his food or letting you walk through the doorway first.

Before beginning your training sessions, you may want to consider putting a collar and leash on your dog. This way you can prevent him from walking off should he get distracted or try to avoid training. You can use either positive reinforcement alone, or a combination of positive and negative reinforcement to teach your Tibetan Mastiff how to sit.

To use positive reinforcement, wave a treat in front of your dog's face to gain his attention. Once he's focused on the treat, raise it slightly above his head and give him the command "sit". You want to hold it out of reach, but not so high that he tries to jump for it. Most dogs will understand that if they sit, they'll be in a position to reach the treat. The moment his hind end touches the ground, be sure to give him the treat immediately and praise him.

To incorporate negative reinforcement into your training, you can try placing your hand on his hips and applying gentle pressure as you move the treat above his head. This will further encourage him to set his hind end down. You can also try putting gentle upward pressure on the leash as you give your verbal command and move the treat into position.

Lie Down

After teaching your Tibetan Mastiff to sit, you can move on to teaching him to lie down. This is a useful command to use in the car, at the vet, or when you have guests in your home. You can also use it to teach your dog tricks like roll over or crawl if your dog is inclined to learn additional commands.

To teach the lie down command, ask your Tibetan Mastiff to sit. Once he's in position, give him the verbal command "lie down" or "down" and lure him to the ground with a treat. Most dogs will follow the treat without lifting their hind end, but some dogs may try to stand up while they put their noses to the ground. If your dog does stand up, simply return him to the sit position and try again. It may take a few repetitions for him to understand what you're asking but be sure to reward him the moment his front end touches the ground.

Recall

The recall command is one of the most important commands that your Tibetan Mastiff will learn. However, it's important to understand that Tibetan Mastiffs may not always obey a recall command if they are distracted or focused on something other than you. Again, Tibetan Mastiffs are not easy dogs to train, and even if your dog responds to your recall command once in a while, it's unlikely that he will respond every time. For this reason, it's important to always have your Tibetan Mastiff on a leash outside your home or fenced property. To teach your dog the recall command, it's helpful to ask a friend or family member to assist you.

If you've already taught your Tibetan Mastiff to recognize his name, he'll already have a basic grasp of this task. Start in an enclosed area with few distractions, such as inside your house in a quiet room. If you're practicing outside, you can also invest in an extra-long leash, or tracking lead, to keep your dog safe while you work. Ask your helper to hold your dog while you walk some distance away with a handful of treats. Say your dog's name to attract his attention and give him the verbal command, "Come!" as you excited pat your legs and encourage him to come see you.

After you give the command, your helper can release the dog so that he can run to you. When he reaches you, be sure to praise him enthusiastically. The more over the top you can be with your praise, the more you'll encourage your dog to participate. Now that your dog is with you, you can hold him while your helper calls him over. This game can be played back and forth and the distance between you and your helper can be increased to present your dog with more of a challenge.

Off

In order to properly enforce the rules of the house, you must teach your Tibetan Mastiff to get off the furniture when asked. However, it's important that you differentiate between this command and the one you use to get your dog to lie down. Many trainers choose "off" to get their dogs off the furniture and "down" to get them to lie down. It doesn't matter what your command is, as long as you are clear about what you are asking when you use it.

There are several different methods you can use to teach the off command. First, you can use positive reinforcement only. To do so, give your verbal command as you lure your Tibetan Mastiff off the furniture. Once all four feet are on the ground, you can reward him with treats and praise.

You can also combine positive and negative reinforcement to teach this command. One method requires your dog to be wearing a leash or slip lead. Apply gentle pressure to the leash as you lure your dog toward the edge of the furniture. If you've been working on leash skills, your dog should understand what you're asking and not brace against the pressure. Again, once all four feet are on the ground, you can reward him.

You can also apply pressure from behind him with your hand, but it's important to use caution when using this method. Dogs that display resource guarding behavior may snap, so if your Tibetan Mastiff has any behavioral issues, you may want to use a method that keeps your hands at a distance. Using your hand to grab your dog's collar to pull him off may also put you at risk, so use your best judgement when deciding how to teach the off command.

Drop It

It's essential that you teach your Tibetan Mastiff to drop items on command that he has picked up with his mouth. Whether it's a chew toy or something he found on a walk, he needs to learn to give it up when asked. Dogs who practice this command regularly are also less likely to develop resource guarding issues.

If your Tibetan Mastiff has something in his mouth, it's never advisable to just take it from him. He may not let go and in some cases may even snap at you. The best way to get something away from your dog and teach him to drop items on command is to offer a trade. First, decide what command you will use. Most trainers use "give" or "drop", but use whatever command works for you. When offering your dog a trade, it's important to use something that your dog considers high value. For instance, if your Tibetan Mastiff is chewing on a delicious bone and you offer him a toy that he doesn't play with much, he's probably not going to accept the trade. However, if it were the other way around, your dog would gladly drop the toy in exchange for the bone.

As you offer the new, high-value item, give your verbal command. You may need to lure your dog away from the item you're trying to get away from him, especially if he's known for resource guarding. Once he drops the old item, reward him immediately with plenty of praise and the new treat or toy. If this is an item he's allowed to have, you can give it right back to him and repeat the process for practice.

Leave It

As you walk your Tibetan Mastiff around the neighborhood or as you give him more freedom in your home, you'll need to teach him to leave certain things alone. Whether it's another dog or a tempting trashcan, your new dog will need to learn to walk away.

Decide what command you want to use for this task. Many trainers choose to use either "leave it" or "walk away". You'll need to have plenty of treats on-hand to teach this command, so be prepared. It can also be helpful to have your dog on a leash so that he can't walk away from you. As your dog becomes focused on something interesting, even if it's not prohibited, wave a treat in front his face to gain his attention. As he becomes focused on the treat, give him the verbal command and encourage him to walk away from whatever was distracting him. After a step or two in the right direction, reward him enthusiastically. As your Tibetan Mastiff progresses, you can ask him to walk further away from a distraction before rewarding him.

Advanced Commands

As your Tibetan Mastiff progresses in his training, you can increase the challenge of his training sessions. If you plan on showing your Tibetan Mastiff, you may need to teach him specific commands in order for him to perform well in the show ring. You can also try teaching him tricks such as shake or roll over. Tibetan Mastiffs need daily mental stimulation, so don't be afraid to get creative. Just remember that your Tibetan Mastiff may not always be interested in learning what you're trying to teach him.

Whatever you choose to teach your new dog, be sure to keep training sessions short and interesting. Your Tibetan Mastiff may lose focus if your sessions go beyond what his attention span can handle. At that point, your session may become difficult and frustrating. This can leave a lasting impression on your dog and he may be less enthusiastic about your next session. Rather than frustrating him, try to keep sessions short and end on a good note. If he seems to be struggling with a certain command or task, try returning to something he knows so that you can reward him and make him feel good about himself. The more positive reinforcement you can provide, the more likely your Tibetan Mastiff is to listen to you. The happier you keep your Tibetan Mastiff during training, the more willing he's going to be to work with you.

CHAPTER 13
Nutrition

The Importance of a Balanced Diet

Ahealthy and nutritious diet is essential to your Tibetan Mastiff's overall health and wellbeing. Without the nutrients provided by a balanced diet, your new family member is at risk of developing serious and sometimes life-threatening conditions. This is especially true if you've brought home a puppy rather than an adult dog. Puppies need a precise balance of fats, proteins, carbohydrates, and amino acids in order for their growing bodies to develop properly. One of the biggest problems with feeding an unbalanced diet is that the effects are not immediate. You may not know for weeks or even months how an improperly balanced diet is affecting your dog, but the consequences are often permanent.

A properly balanced diet does not only mean a diet that has the proper ratios of nutrients, but an ideal number of calories for your dog's age and activity level. Obesity is by far the most common diet-related problem faced by domestic dogs. Portion control is as much of a crucial aspect of a proper diet as the food itself. Growing puppies and active adults are likely to need more calories than a senior or sedentary adult dog. Many types of pet food

Photo Courtesy
of Nicole Moss

Photo Courtesy
of Zdenek Neuman

have a table displayed on the bag of suggested calories based on your dog's weight, but these are merely a suggestion. You should feed your dog according to his individual needs, not the chart on the dog food packaging. If you are unsure of how much your Tibetan Mastiff should be eating or if he's at a healthy weight, you should consult your veterinarian for advice.

As you browse your local pet store's dog food aisles, you may notice that some pet food companies label their food as being appropriate for dogs of all life stages. For some dogs, these types of food may be appropriate, but others may need a more specialized diet. Often, large breed puppies need a more specialized diet than smaller breeds to ensure slow and even growth. As your dog ages or develops health problems, you may also need to adjust his diet accordingly. It's important to understand that you may not be able to feed your dog the same food for his entire life.

Basic Nutrition

Canine nutrition is an incredibly complex topic in which most owners, and indeed many veterinary professionals, choose to learn only the basics. Certified canine nutritionists, on the other hand spend their lives studying nutrition and attempting to improve the ways we feed our beloved pets. This section will cover only the very basics of nutrition, but if you have any questions about how or what to feed your dog, the American College of Veterinary Nutrition (ACVN) provides a list of board certified veterinary nutritionists on their website that are available for consultation.

Proteins and Amino Acids

Simply put, amino acids are organic compounds that when combined form proteins. This means that when protein molecules are broken down or digested, the amino acids remain. Your dog uses these amino acids to synthesize protein molecules within the body, which aid in cell growth, maintenance, and repair. For example, up to 30 percent of your Tibetan Mastiff's daily protein intake goes toward the maintenance of his fur cells.

Proteins are made up of approximately 20 amino acids and about half of these are produced internally by your dog's body. The other half are often referred to as "essential amino acids" and must be provided by the dog's diet. These amino acids are considered essential because if one is deficient, the body will be unable to make certain proteins effectively. The protein building process is essentially stopped in its tracks.

10 Essential Amino Acids

- Arginine
- Lysine
- Tryptophan
- Histidine
- Methionine
- Valine
- Isoleucine
- Phenylalanine
- Leucine
- Threonine

Fortunately, foods such as meat, eggs, and dairy products are high in protein, which provides your dog's body the right proportions of amino acids for protein synthesis. Plants, on the other hand, tend to be low in protein and will not provide enough protein to maintain proper protein synthesis. This is why vegetarian and vegan diets are not biologically appropriate for dogs.

Fat and Fatty Acids

The most concentrated source of energy in your Tibetan Mastiff's diet comes from fats. Fats also provide your dog with fatty acids, which are similar to amino acids in that they are the building blocks for important substances in the body that are required for cell growth and maintenance. Fats also aid in the absorption of fat-soluble vitamins such as A, E, D, and K. Additionally, fats tend to make food more palatable, so high fat diets may appeal more to picky eaters than low fat diets. Like amino acids, there are a few fatty acids that are essential to your dog's diet and must be provided by his food.

Essential Fatty Acids

- Linoleic acid
- Linolenic acid
- Arachidonic acid

If you have a basic understanding of nutrition, you may be familiar with omega-3 and omega-6 fatty acids. Within your dog's diet, linoleic acid is the source of omega-6 fatty acids, while linolenic acid provides your dog with omega-3 fatty acids. A properly balanced diet will provide more omega-6 than omega-3 fatty acids, typically at a 4 to 1 ratio.

Carbohydrates

Although carbohydrates provide your dog with some energy, dogs do not necessary require them in their diet. This is why many raw feeders choose to feed their dogs little to no grains or vegetables. Carbohydrates provide energy for your Tibetan Mastiff's body when they are broken down by the digestive system into glucose. Additionally, carbohydrates such as grains provide your dog with additional nutrients such as iron, antioxidants, phytochemicals, and other minerals, as well as fiber. Most starchy carbohydrates will need to well cooked in order for dogs to be able to properly digest them. Otherwise, they may ferment in the large intestine.

Feeding Dogs at Different Life Stages

As your Tibetan Mastiff grows and develops, his nutritional needs will change. As your dog's needs change, you'll need to adjust his diet accordingly to maintain optimum health. Although foods marketed as being appropriate for all life stages are fine for many dogs, many owners choose to feed according to their dog's current life stage. For example, as a growing puppy, your dog will require a higher level of calories, as well as a specific ratio of vitamins and minerals such as phosphate and calcium. Large breed puppies are at a higher risk of developing orthopedic problems, such as hip dysplasia, if their diet isn't providing them with the nutrients needed for slow and even growth. Feeding a diet designed for slow growth won't limit your dog's mature size, but it will allow him to take his time in getting there rather than growing faster than his joints can manage.

As your dog reaches maturity, his caloric requirements will be reduced, at which point you will likely switch from puppy food to adult food. Typically, this occurs when your dog has reached about 80% of his predicted adult size, usually at around 12 months of age. During adulthood, your Tibetan Mastiff's nutritional needs may change according to his activity level and any health problems he may develop. Additionally, dogs who have not

Photo Courtesy of Maria Folkomina

been spayed or neutered typically require more calories than those who have been altered. Pregnant and lactating females will also require different nutrients to aid in the proper development and growth of their puppies.

When your Tibetan Mastiff has reached his senior years, usually around six to eight years of age or so, you will want to consider switching him to a senior formula. Senior foods are similar to adult maintenance formulas, but often contain lower levels of fat to help prevent excess weight gain and increased levels of antioxidants. Moderate levels of protein will also help maintain muscle mass, but without overworking your dog's kidneys. If your Tibetan Mastiff develops any health problems, such as heart disease, diabetes, or arthritis, you may need to adjust his diet accordingly.

Photo Courtesy of Olga Kiseleva

Burgundiy Chelenger Iz Chentao-Park, 4 months, TZAR - Owned by R. Eichorn & E. Valle.

Different Types of Commercial Food

When you think of commercial dog food, the first thing that probably comes to mind is a bowl of brown crunchy nuggets. Kibble is by far the most popular type of commercial dog food due to its convenience and the nearly endless range of options. Kibble is available in different formulas specifically created for dogs of different life stages and health needs. Some companies even offer specific formulas targeting different breeds. As instances of food allergies and sensitivities increase, many companies have answered the call with novel proteins such as salmon, duck, and kangaroo. Kibble is available in a range of sizes, from petite pieces made for toy breeds to giant pieces designed to help clean your dog's teeth. If your dog suffers from a specific condition such as arthritis, kidney, or heart disease, you will be able to find a kibble suited to his nutritional needs. However, many kibbles formulated to help specific health issues are only available from a veterinarian.

Corn, wheat, and soy can cause digestive or allergy issues with some dogs, so many owners are switching to grain-free diets where traditional grains are replaced by other carbohydrates, such as potatoes and peas. Some veterinarians caution against the use of grain-free kibble, however, due to the correlation between this type of food and dilated cardiomyopathy (DCM). DCM is a heart condition and definitive causes have been a subject of debate. The connection between grain-free kibble and DCM has not yet been proven, but research is ongoing. If you have concerns about feeding grain-free kibble or DCM, it's best to discuss this with your veterinarian.

Regardless of formula, kibble is a great choice for owners who lack the time or money to make their dog's food at home. Foods containing limited ingredients and those requiring a prescription from your vet may be more expensive, but kibble is available at a wide variety of price points to suit any budget.

Canned food is another popular commercial dog food. It's softer and smells stronger than kibble, so it's an ideal choice for senior dogs or picky eaters. Canned food is available in nearly as many options as kibble, so if your Tibetan Mastiff has specific nutritional needs, you should be able to find a canned food to suit him. Canned food also contains more moisture than kibble, so it's often a great choice for dogs who drink less water than they should to stay hydrated. It should be noted that some canned food is more calorie dense than kibble, so you'll need to monitor portions closely. One downside to canned food is that it often adheres to dogs' teeth, so you may need to brush your dog's teeth more frequently or provide him with more dental chews or toys. Professional dental cleanings may also need to be scheduled more frequently for dogs on strict canned food diets.

Recently, fresh-cooked dog food has become popular with dog owners who like the idea of homecooked diets but lack the time or means to make their dog's food. Like canned food, fresh-cooked food is softer than kibble so it may be ideal for picky dogs or those with dental problems. You can usually find this type of food in the refrigerated section of your local pet store. It's typically packaged into rolls, which can be sliced into appropriately sized portions and returned to the fridge until the next meal. Fresh-cooked food is often more expensive than kibble or canned food diets, so you may want to consider your budget before starting your dog on this type of food.

As more owners begin to see the benefits of feeding their dogs species appropriate diets, commercial raw dog food is rising in popularity. Found in your local pet store's freezer section, raw dog food is typically comprised of a nutritionally balanced mixture of meat, organs, bones, and vegetables. Raw foods do not contain grains and are usually quite low in carbohydrates. They are available in a wide variety of proteins to accommodate dogs with allergies or sensitivities. Commercial raw diets are typically formed into either small nuggets or larger patties to suit dogs of all sizes. Most raw feeders compliment their dog's diet with recreational raw bones to give their dogs the chance to clean their teeth as they chew. Many owners also choose to supplement their dog's raw diet with other ingredients found in the freezer sections such as goat's milk and bone broth.

Homemade Diets

Some Tibetan Mastiff owners choose to make their dog's food rather than feed him a commercially made diet. Depending on the area you live in and the ingredients you use, homemade diets may be more expensive than traditional kibble or canned food. Homemade food is also more labor intensive, so it's crucial that you consider your both your budget and your schedule when deciding whether to make your dog's food. Commercial diets are required by law to meet certain nutritional standards, but homemade foods do not, so you must be certain that what you are feeding your dog is nutritionally balanced. Remember, diet imbalances will not show up right away and you may not see the long-term effects on your dog's health until it's too late. If you're not sure whether your homemade dog food is nutritionally balanced, speak with your veterinarian. Certified pet nutritionists are also great resources for formulating and evaluating homemade diets.

Raw diets are probably the most popular types of homemade diets and can typically be divided into two categories. The first is referred to as Prey Model Raw (PMR) and is typically formulated according to the estimated percentages of meat, bone, and organ within a prey animal. PMR diets usually consist of around 80% muscle meat, 10% bone, and 10% organ. Some owners may supplement a PMR diet with a small amount of vegetables and fruit, but some do not.

The other category of raw diet, Biologically Appropriate Raw Food (BARF), is similar to PMR but typically allows for more vegetables and carbohydrates. Regardless of the type of raw diet, many owners also add supplements such as goat's milk, fish stock, and bone broth to provide their dogs with a wealth of additional nutrients. As raw diets typically contain a certain amount of bone, some owners may choose to grind or process their dog's food while others allow their dogs to chew the bones themselves.

Cooked diets are also popular, particularly with dogs who cannot tolerate a raw diet. Cooked diets are also safer for families with members whose immune systems may be compromised and should not be exposed to any potential pathogens in raw meat. The ingredients of cooked homemade diets are similar to raw diets, but the ingredients are usually baked or boiled. Some cooked diets also contain more carbohydrates, such as barley or rice. To make up for nutrition lost to the high temperatures of cooking, some diets may be supplemented with ingredients such as kelp, vitamin mixtures, or dairy products. As cooked bones cannot be fed, calcium must be provided through the addition of other sources, such as ground eggshells or calcium powder.

It's important to understand that safety precautions must be taken when feeding your dog bones in a homemade diet. Raw bones do not shatter the same way that cooked bones do, so if you do choose to feed your dog a homemade diet, you must be certain that you only provide him with raw bones and never offer him cooked bones. Cooked bones may splinter and may become lodged in your dog's throat or puncture him internally. Harder, weight-bearing bones such as leg bones may also need to be avoided. Although some owners use these as recreational chews for their dogs, these bones may present a hazard for heavy chewers. Dogs who are intense chewers can easily break a tooth on such hard bones. Some dogs may also need to be monitored when chewing bones or have bones ground into their food if they have a history of gulping their food. Some dogs may learn to be patient and chew their food while others may be lifelong gulpers. As your dog's guardian it's your responsibility to understand his nature and adjust his food accordingly.

If you choose to make your Tibetan Mastiff's food, you need to be certain that you are feeding a properly balanced diet. There are many books available that can teach you the basics of canine nutrition. You may also want to consult a canine nutritionist. Most nutritionists are happy to provide you with a balanced recipe or evaluate your homemade diet for a nominal fee. Recipes are tailored to your dog's nutritional needs based on his size, age, activity level, and health concerns. Ingredients are often chosen according to budget and availability. Canine nutritionists often consult a variety of resources when formulating recipes for clients, including the National Research Council (NRC) or Association of American Feed Control (AAFCO) to ensure that their recipes are properly balanced.

Weight Management

Obesity is among the most common health concerns in modern pets. According to the Association of Pet Obesity Prevention, approximately 52 percent of dogs in the United States are considered overweight or obese and more than 90 percent of owners do not recognize that their dogs weigh more than they should. Obesity can lead to a multitude of other health problems and severely limit your dog's ability to play and enjoy his life. Excess weight is incredibly hard on joints, especially those of puppies and seniors, and can quickly lead to arthritis and other joint problems. It can be tempting to toss your beloved pup a treat every time he asks for it, but for the sake of his health, you must resist. In addition to properly managing your dog's weight at home, you should discuss your dog's weight with your veterinarian at every opportunity. Your vet will be able to evaluate your Tibetan Mastiff's weight and advise you on any dietary or lifestyle changes that should be made.

Portion sizes are one of the biggest factors in keeping your Tibetan Mastiff at a healthy weight. Making sure your dog is getting just the right amount at each mealtime is important, but you also need to factor in his daily allotment of treats and edible chews. It's easy to forget that handful of treats you give your dog during every training session, but those calories will go straight to his waistline if you aren't careful. If you're worried about your dog's weight, you can always use a portion of his daily meals as training treats. You can also substitute high calorie treats for healthy options such as chopped vegetables or fruit. Fruit should be fed in moderation, however, due to its high sugar content.

Remember, the more calories your Tibetan Mastiff burns, the more food he can eat. If you're worried about your dog's weight but don't want to feed him any less, than you need to increase his daily activity. Longer walks and more frequent play sessions will not only keep your dog at a healthy weight, but it will keep both his mind and body fit.

Food Allergies and Intolerances

As with humans, dogs can sometimes develop food allergies or intolerances. Allergies and intolerances differ in that allergies are a response from your dog's immune system to a certain protein in your dog's diet, while intolerances are digestive upset or poor digestion due to a certain ingredient. Depending on the severity of the reaction, symptoms of food allergies can include itching, hot spots, ear or

HELPFUL TIP
The Importance of High-Quality Food

Since Tibetan Mastiffs can be prone to bone and joint problems, it's crucial to keep them at a healthy weight. Look for dog food that has animal protein as the first ingredient and avoid foods that contain corn, soy, wheat, or animal by-products.

skin infections, diarrhea, and vomiting. Dog food ingredients that are commonly to blame for reactions include beef, chicken, corn, wheat, and soy, though dogs may be reactive to any ingredient in their food.

Although there are tests available for food sensitivities, they are not always reliable. Therefore, many veterinarians suggest using elimination diets to determine the source of the problem. Elimination diets are performed by starting the dog on a diet with a novel protein, such as salmon or kangaroo. Few dogs are allergic to novel proteins, so they're assumed to be a safe place to start. Once symptoms have been eliminated with a dietary change, other proteins are introduced one at a time. If the dog does not react to a certain protein, another is introduced. If the dog does react, then you will know what protein or ingredient you need to avoid. Remember, your dog cannot have any treats or extra food while on an elimination diet as you do not know whether they are the cause of your dog's symptoms.

Some veterinarians also recommend hypoallergenic diets, which are typically available only by prescription. Hypoallergenic diets are typically formulated using hydrolyzed proteins, meaning that the proteins have been broken down into a size that is unlikely to trigger a response to the immune system. Prescription diets tend to be quite expensive, so if budgetary limits are a concern, you may want to perform an elimination diet before you resort to a hypoallergenic diet.

CHAPTER 14
Physical and Mental Exercise

"They need a good sized yard to run in and usually will exercise themselves by running along the fence-line as they are patrolling their property. We find that a dog that gets more exercise is much more relaxed and a better companion."

__Michael Brantley__
Dreamland Kennel

The Importance of Physical Exercise

One of the most obvious benefits of physical exercise is weight control. Physical activity is essential in managing your Tibetan Mastiff's weight. Without enough exercise, your dog may become overweight, which will put excess strain on his joints. This strain can be especially damaging to puppies, whose joints are still growing and developing, and senior dogs, who may be developing painful arthritis. There are also myriad other weight-related conditions that can be avoided with the right combination of physical exercise and portion control.

Physical activity will also allow your Tibetan Mastiff to exercise his mind. While a walk around the neighborhood may not seem like much of a mental exercise, it's far more than he would experience laying around on the sofa all day. The new sights and smells will keep his mind active and stimulated. Without this essential mental activity, your dog may look for other ways to entertain himself, usually by destroying something around the house. Richard Eichhorn of Drakyi Tibetan Mastiffs advises, "This boredom can lead to destructive and disruptive behavior that can result in personality problems." Remember, a tired dog is a content and quiet dog, so be sure to keep your Tibetan Mastiff busy.

Just how much physical exercise you give your Tibetan Mastiff each day will depend on a few factors. His age, energy, and overall health will determine how much exercise he actually needs. Most dogs will do well with between one and two hours of exercise each day. This does not mean you

*Photo Courtesy
of Dani Allen Smith*

HELPFUL TIP
Boredom = Destruction

Tibetan Mastiffs were bred to guard a large property all night long. Without a similar job to do, they can become bored and destruc¬tive. Make sure your Tibetan is getting plenty of exercise and mental stimulation to prevent them from being destructive to your home and yard.

need to take your dog for two hour walks every day. This time-frame can include walking, hiking, playtime, or even training sessions and can be split up into different sessions throughout the day. Obviously, puppies and older dogs will have less stamina than healthy adults, so they'll do best with more frequent short sessions. Most owners will find success in providing their dog with an exercise session in the morning before they leave for work and another when they return home in the evening. While some owners prefer a shorter session in the morning and a longer one in the evening, you may find that more exercise before you leave will help your dog to rest quietly in your absence.

Exercising Puppies

"Be sure YOU are the trainer of our own Tibetan Mastiff. Use advice from professional trainers, but don't have them try to train your dog. After your puppy has all its vaccinations at 4 months, take them on daily walks."

George Pragmateftakis
Phantasmagoria Tibetan Mastiffs

Dogs younger than about 18 months of age should not take part in strenuous levels of activity as it can be damaging to their growing bodies. This does not mean you can't exercise them; it simply means that you should be cautious about how long or how far you go with them. Tibetan Mastiffs are a slow growing breed, so it's best to use caution until your dog reaches maturity at around 18-24 months of age. Rather than taking your dog hiking for several hours at a time, break your walks up into shorter, more manageable sessions.

Training sessions should also be kept short due to your growing puppy's short attention span. Typically, sessions as short as five to fifteen minutes are ideal. These sessions can be repeated as frequently as every few

Photo Courtesy
of Nathaniel Askins

hours if necessary. It's important to quit before your dog loses focus, so if you notice your dog's attention drifting after about seven minutes of training, try to quit at around five minutes. The more strenuous and frustrating the sessions are, the less likely it is that your dog will look forward to the next one.

The most important aspect of exercising your Tibetan Mastiff puppy is to allow him to set his own limits. If he enjoys playing for 20 minutes at a time, you can allow him to do so, but don't expect to take him on a four-hour long hike through the mountains. Most puppies have a good understanding of what they can handle and will gladly let you know when they've had enough.

The Importance of Mental Exercise

As previously mentioned, mental stimulation is crucial in preventing your Tibetan Mastiff from seeking entertainment through the destruction of your home. Tibetan Mastiffs love to chew and will gladly chew up your furniture and belongings in the absence of other activities. Of course, mental exercise won't guarantee the safety of your sofa, but it will reduce the likelihood of your dog resorting to his own methods of entertainment.

Mental exercise is especially important for dogs who are unable to get enough physical exercise due to health or mobility problems. Puppies and senior dogs may benefit more from mental exercise, simply because their bodies are limited on how much physical activity they can handle. Challenging toys, games, and activities involving interesting scents will engage your dog's mind and allow him to stimulate his mind without overworking his body.

It's important to note that most dogs will find mental exercise far more exhausting than physical exercise. Your dog may be able to play for hours at a time but will become tired after just ten to fifteen minutes of strenuous mental work. This is normal, so plan on keeping your training sessions short and focus on just one or two tasks at a time. Pushing your Tibetan Mastiff beyond his mental limit will only frustrate him and he may be less willing to work with you in future sessions.

Tibetan Mastiffs as Athletes

There are many different types of dog sports available to owners and their companions, but unfortunately, there are very few that Tibetan Mastiffs truly enjoy. Tibetan Mastiffs are athletic dogs, but most do not enjoy competing in sports. Some owners may still find joy in teaching their dogs various aspects of different sports. Your Tibetan Mastiff may enjoy going through weave poles or over small jumps, but he may be completely uninterested in completing an entire agility course. This is not to say your Tibetan Mastiff will never be able to compete in an agility or obedience ring, but you will need to be realistic about your expectations. Tibetan Mastiffs are quite independent dogs who would rather do their own thing than compete in organized dog sports, so you may need to adapt your dog's training to suit his own individual preferences.

Even if you don't compete in dog sports, there are still plenty of activities you can enjoy with your Tibetan Mastiff. If you enjoy long, scenic walks or hikes, your Tibetan Mastiff may gladly accompany you. Some Tibetan Mastiffs may also enjoy swimming. Part of Tibetan Mastiff ownership involves getting to know your dog and adapting his exercise needs to what he likes to do, so don't be afraid to experiment and see what activities he does and does not enjoy.

Photo Courtesy of Barbara Wolf

Double Eye Sansibar

Playtime

There are many different types of playtime through which your Tibetan Mastiff can get his daily physical and mental exercise. Some dogs prefer a certain type of play, while others will play with anyone and everyone. If your dog enjoys playing during his alone time, you can provide him with a variety of toys. Most Tibetan Mastiffs will enjoy the satisfaction of a good chew toy, but you might also try toys with food or treats hidden inside. Rubber chew toys, such as a Kong, can be filled with everything from kibble to frozen yogurt to provide a mentally stimulating treat. You might also try puzzle toys, which can be made out of either wood or plastic. Puzzle toys typically have various flaps, sliding doors, and cups that must be moved by your dog's nose or paw in order to reach the food inside. As puzzle toys come in different levels of difficulty, many owners opt to buy a few to rotate so that their dog always has a new challenge.

Some Tibetan Mastiffs prefer playtime with another dog. If your Tibetan Mastiff is an only dog, you might try setting up playdates with friends or family members who own friendly and playful dogs. Regular play sessions with other dogs are not only a great way to keep your dog mentally and physically stimulated, but it's an excellent way to socialize him. The more

frequently you can provide your dog with playdates, the happier and calmer he'll be. However, it's important to only set up playdates with dogs that you know and trust and play must always be supervised for safety reasons.

If you would prefer a more hands-on approach to playtime with your Tibetan Mastiff, don't be afraid to take a more active approach to his play. Whether it's a good game of chase, tug, or even fetch if he's so inclined, your Tibetan Mastiff will love spending time with you. Some owners also choose to incorporate treats into their playtime by hiding them around the yard or house and having the dog find the treats through his sense of smell. This scavenger hunt style game is an ideal way to mentally stimulate your dog without overworking his body, so it's great for puppies and older dogs.

Remember, your Tibetan Mastiff is an individual, so the type of play he enjoys may not be the same as someone else's Tibetan Mastiff. Don't be afraid to experiment with different types of play to see what he enjoys. It's also possible that your Tibetan Mastiff may prefer other types of physical or mental exercise, so don't despair if he doesn't appreciate the new squeaky toys you've purchased for him. Tibetan Mastiffs simply prefer to do things on their own terms, so your dog will certainly let you know if he's not enjoying an activity.

CHAPTER 15
Grooming

Coat Basics

One of the most recognizable characteristics of the Tibetan Mastiff is their heavy double coat. A proper coat consists of a thick wooly undercoat and coarse outer guard hairs. Although the coat is fairly long all over the dog's body, males especially will have a particularly heavy "mane" around their neck. However, despite all this fur, the Tibetan Mastiff's coat is relatively low maintenance for most of the year. During the winter, weekly brushing and monthly bathing should be enough to keep your Tibetan Mastiff looking and feeling great. However, as warm weather approaches, Tibetan Mastiffs "blow" their undercoats as a way to shed

Photo Courtesy
of Richard Eichhorn
Drakyi Tibetan Mastiffs

GCH Drakyi Bravado, BRAVO, at 16 months

their winter warmth and pre-pare for summer. During this period, expect to spend more time than usual caring for your dog's coat.

HELPFUL TIP
Nonshedding

Tibetan Mastiffs don't shed much through most of the year. Instead, they "blow" their under-coat once a year, usually in the spring, resulting in hair everywhere. They still need weekly brushing through the year and daily brushing when they blow their coat.

The Tibetan Mastiff's coat developed as a way to pro-tect them from harsh Tibet-an winter weather. However, this does not mean that they can only live in colder climates. The breed is perfectly capa-ble of handling hot weather. Richard Eichhorn of Drakyi Tibetan Mas-tiffs says, "Since they shed out most of their coat by early summer, they seem to endure dry heat quite well. When temperatures reach 80+ de-grees, the Tibetan Mastiff's activity level is greatly reduced during the day and food consumption can drop 25-50 percent." However, if you live in a hot, humid climate, you may need to rethink your choice of breed. Richard Eichhorn adds, "Generally speaking, the Tibetan Mastiff is adapt-able to almost any climate and its coat develops accordingly. However, we don't recommend the dogs be kept in a tropical climate where ex-treme heat and humidity are factors unless indoor air-conditioned facil-ities are available to the dog at all times. Being that Tibetan Mastiffs do have a longer, thicker double coat, they do not thrive and are lethargic in extreme humidity."

The coat of the Tibetan Mastiff should not be trimmed or cut. Their coat is designed to insulate them from both the cold weather of win-ter and the heat of summer. Under no circumstances should a Tibet-an Mastiff's coat be shaved. Not only does this remove their protective insulation, but it may permanently damage their coat. Double coats that have been shaved typically do not grow back correctly, usually with an incorrect balance of too much undercoat and not enough guard hairs. According to the breed standard, the only trimming that is al-lowed in the show ring is a light tidying of the feet and hocks to give a clean appearance.

Essential Grooming Tools

One of best tools for brushing your Tibetan Mastiff and preventing mats is a wire slicker brush or metal rake comb. Slicker brushes and rakes are ideal for separating the coat to prevent mats, loosen dead hair, and remove dirt and debris. Slicker brushes come in different sizes, firmness of the bristles, and handle shapes, so choose one that appeals to you. Rakes are also available in a variety of shapes and sizes, but you'll need to choose one with teeth long enough to reach through the Tibetan Mastiff's heavy coat. They're easy to use, even for owners who are inexperienced with grooming their own dogs. It can be difficult to be sure that you're brushing all the way through a particularly thick coat though, so be sure that your brush strokes are reaching down to the skin without scratching or scraping.

To make sure that you're brushing your dog's entire coat, professional groomers recommend checking your work with a metal comb. Metal combs may be referred to as 'greyhound combs' and come with different teeth lengths. They may or may not have a handle. Choose a comb that fits well in your hand and has enough space between the teeth to run smoothly through

Photo Courtesy of Draky Tibetan Mastiffs

CH Drakyi Gold Standard, MIDAS. Owned by R. Eichhorn, Michael & Linda Brantley

Photo Courtesy of Nikki Love

your dog's coat. Combs tend to reach farther into a heavy coat and will easily snag on any tangles or mats hiding deep inside. Many groomers start with a slicker brush to detangle the coat and then go over everything once more with a comb to make sure there are no mats or tangles left behind.

You may also want to invest in a dematting tool. Dematting tools come in a variety of shapes and sizes and may have one or more blades. These blades are designed to be inserted into the coat just below a mat and gently pulled through to loosen and break up the mat. However, it's important to note that the blades can be sharp, so handle them gently to prevent injury to you or your dog. If you're not sure how to use a dematter effectively, don't be afraid to ask your local groomer for advice.

If you plan on trimming your Tibetan Mastiff's nails yourself, you'll want to buy a nail trimmer or grinder. If you choose a trimmer over a grinder, most groomers will recommend scissor-style trimmers over guillotine-style trimmers. Scissor-type nail trimmers tend to make cleaner cuts through even the toughest nails, while guillotine-style trimmers can sometimes crush the nail rather than cut through it. Grinders are rising in popularity, however, due to their ease of use and minimal discomfort for the dog. Since grinders simply file the nail down, there's no uncomfortable pressure on the nail like with trimmers. Whether you choose a trimmer or grinder will depend on your own preference as well as your dog's. Some dogs may prefer one over the other, but most will adapt to whatever tool you may choose to use.

Bathing

Due to the Tibetan Mastiff's low maintenance coat, you won't need to spend much time bathing your new dog. Richard Eichhorn of Drakyi Tibetan Mastiffs advises, "Since this breed has no doggy odor, bathing more than once a month is neither recommended nor required." Bathing too frequently can dry out the coat and skin, causing irritation and dandruff. On the other hand, not bathing your dog frequently enough can allow excess dirt and oil to build up, which can cause skin problems as well.

There are many different types of dog shampoo on the market and which one you use will depend on the condition of your Tibetan Mastiff's coat as well as your own preference. If your dog has any issues such as itchiness, sensitive skin, or he's blowing his coat, you should be able to find an appropriate shampoo. Likewise, if you prefer shampoos with more subtle or perhaps fruity scents, your local pet store or favorite online retailer should have just what you're looking for. Try to find a shampoo with more natural ingredients to reduce the likelihood of skin irritation. It should be noted that many natural ingredient-based shampoos will produce far fewer bubbles than those with chemicals designed to produce suds. A lack of bubbles does not mean your dog won't be clean when you're done.

Some owners choose to follow their shampoo of choice with a conditioner, but conditioner is not always necessary. For dogs who are shedding heavily or have coats that mat frequently, conditioner can be beneficial, but it can often take longer for the coat to dry. Most dogs with healthy coats don't need conditioner or can get by with a simple leave-in spray conditioner afterwards.

When bathing your Tibetan Mastiff, it's crucial that you get the shampoo down to the skin. If you only wash the hair on top, you're leaving enough dirt, oil, and dead skin to cause irritation and mats below the clean hair. It can sometimes be difficult to bathe dogs with especially thick coats, so you may want to try shampooing your dog in sections and parting the hair as you go. Bathing systems, such as the Hydrosurge, are designed to help push shampoo and water through even the thickest coats, but they can be expensive. You can also try using a rubber curry brush to help distribute shampoo evenly through the coat, but be careful not to tangle the hair as you go.

As you shampoo your Tibetan Mastiff, it's important that you use caution when scrubbing around his face. Avoid getting shampoo in your dog's ears and eyes. Some groomers have eye rinse on hand, just in case and may put cotton balls in the dog's ears to prevent water from running into the ear canals. If you choose to do this, be sure to remove the cotton balls when you're done. Otherwise, just be careful when shampooing around these delicate areas.

Rinsing is probably the most important aspect of bathing your dog. Shampoo residue left in the coat can lead to skin irritation and even hot spots, so you want to make sure you rinse your Tibetan Mastiff as thoroughly as possible. Most professional groomers will tell you that when you think you've removed all the shampoo from the coat to rinse one more time just to be sure. Once the coat is thoroughly shampoo-free, you can follow up with conditioner if you so choose. Some conditioners need to be left on the coat for a few minutes while others can be rinsed immediately, so be sure to read the directions on the bottle. As with shampoo, conditioner needs to be rinsed completely from the coat.

Professional groomers tend to dry their clients' dogs with a high-velocity dryer. These powerful dryers work to dry the coat down to the skin, while helping to blow out dead skin and hair. This can help cut back on the amount of brushing needed afterward. However, these dryers are loud, sometimes expensive, and may be tricky to handle. If you are interested in using a high-velocity dryer at home, consider asking your local groomer for advice on handling the dryer and teaching your dog to tolerate the process. You may also consider using a handheld dryer, which can be effective in drying the coat, but may take longer than a high velocity dryer. Regardless of the type of dryer you use, be careful if the dryer produces heat as you don't want to burn your dog's skin or hair. Of course, you can also allow your dog's coat to air dry if you choose.

Brushing

Most groomers recommend brushing Tibetan Mastiffs one to three times per week. This is typically enough to keep the coat detangled and prevent mats from developing. However, there are certain times when you may need to brush your dog more frequently. For instance, during the spring or summer, you may need to brush your Tibetan Mastiff as frequently as every day. According to Debbie Mayer of Noble Legacy Tibetan Mastiffs, "This shedding process will last six to eight weeks and requires frequent brushing and combing to prevent mats and tangles." She adds, "If you don't have the time or patience to treat your dog to frequent springtime spa days, this is definitely not the breed for you." The more frequently you brush your dog during this time, the less hair you'll need to vacuum off your floors and furniture.

Most owners choose to start brushing their Tibetan Mastiffs with a wire slicker brush. You will need to be sure to use only light pressure on areas where the brush may come into contact with the skin, however, as the wire bristles can scratch the skin if too much pressure is applied. One of the downsides of the slicker brush is that it can be difficult to ensure that you are brushing through the entire coat. It's common for inexperienced owners to believe they're brushing their dogs thoroughly only to find out that their slicker brush has only been going through the top layer of coat and the undercoat has become matted near the skin.

To ensure even brushing throughout the coat, follow the slicker brush with a metal comb to double check your work. If you run into any mats, try to gently work them out with a dematter. If you run into a particularly difficult mat, you may need to remove it with scissors. Whenever you cut a mat from your dog's coat, you need to use extreme caution so as not to cut the dog's skin. Use round-tipped scissors if possible. Of course, you can always just take your dog to a professional groomer for mat removal as well.

Cleaning Eyes and Ears

Tibetan Mastiffs are not prone to ear infections, but it is a possibility, especially if you neglect your dog's ear care. An infection can happen quickly if a small amount of moisture enters the ear canal. This can happen during a bath or swim, but that moisture combined with your dog's natural body heat creates the ideal environment for yeast and bacteria to thrive. To prevent ear infections, you should clean your Tibetan Mastiff's ears regularly, especially after bathing or swimming. If you notice that your dog seems to

Photo Courtesy
of Nousis Xaralampos

scratch at one or both ears often, or there is redness, swelling, or an unpleasant odor in your dog's ears, he may already have an ear infection. A quick trip to the vet for diagnosis and the appropriate medication will solve the problem before it causes too much discomfort.

There are a variety of ear cleaners on the market, typically categorized into two groups. One type of ear cleaner contains alcohol. Alcohol-based cleaners are often used for post-swim ear cleaning as the alcohol evaporates quickly, removing excess moisture from the ear. However, if your Tibetan Mastiff already has an ear infection, or simply sensitive ears, the alcohol may produce an unpleasant burning sensation. The second category of ear cleaners are non-alcohol based and are designed for use with sensitive or irritated ears.

To clean your Tibetan Mastiff's ears, wet a cotton ball in the ear cleaner of your choice. Squeeze out excess cleaner before inserting the cotton ball into your dog's ears. Using your fingers, wipe around your dog's ear canal. Don't be afraid to go inside, as your finger is big enough that you won't be able to reach down into the sensitive parts of the ear. It's important that you use only your fingers and a cotton ball, rather than a cotton swab. Cotton swabs can reach too far into the ear canal and you can accidentally damage your dog's ear. Fortunately, your finger will be unable to reach any important structures of the ear, so you can clean away without worry. Once you've cleaned away any dirt or excess wax, you can go over the ear again with a clean, dry cotton ball. This will prevent your dog from wiping ear cleaner all over your furniture or floors.

Most Tibetan Mastiffs do not have a problem with tear stains, so cleaning your dog's eyes will rarely be necessary. Some dogs may develop crusty bits of discharge at the corners of their eyes that may need cleaning from time to time. Your local pet store or favorite online retailer likely has a selection of either pre-soaked eye wipes or eye cleaner available. To clean your Tibetan Mastiff's eyes, simply soak a cotton ball in eye cleaner or take a pre-soaked wipe and squeeze out excess cleaning solution. Then, you can simply wipe away any discharge from your dog's eyes. Although this type of cleaner is usually safe for use around the eyes, be careful so that you do not scratch or poke your dog's eyes as you clean.

Trimming Nails

How often you trim your Tibetan Mastiffs nails will depend on a few different factors. Some dogs' nails simply grow faster than others, but if you frequently walk your dog on pavement, you may find that his daily walks keep his nails ground down. If you walk on grass or dirt trails, the surface may not be rough enough to wear down your dog's nails. For some owners, weekly nail trims help keep their dog's nails nice and short, but others may choose to only trim their dog's nails when they receive their monthly bath. Consider how quickly your dog's nails grow and decide what time-frame works best for you. As you get your Tibetan Mastiff used to the nail trimming process, you may want to do it more often just so that he understands what is expected of him more quickly.

Regardless of whether you choose to clip or grind your Tibetan Mastiff's nails, the first step you need to take is to locate the quick of the nail. The quick is the blood supply to the nail and in addition to being painful if cut, it can bleed profusely, so it's important to know where it's at so you can avoid it. With light colored nails, locating the quick is easy, but you may not be able to see it if your dog has dark nails. After brushing aside any hair that may be in the way, trim just a thin layer off your dog's nail to begin with. If you trim your dog's nails frequently, this may be all that is needed. You want to keep an eye out for a darker circle in the middle of your dog's nails. It may take several layers before you begin to see the circle, but once you do, stop! This is your dog's quick and the nail has been trimmed short enough. Repeat this procedure for each of your dog's nails and don't forget about the dewclaws, if your dog has them.

If you are uncomfortable with the idea of trimming your Tibetan Mastiff's nails, or simply don't want to, don't be afraid to ask your veterinarian or groomer to trim them for you. Nail trims are inexpensive, and most vets and groomers offer the option of either clipping or grinding. The professionals are also more adept at handling large or difficult dogs, so they'll be able to do a better job than the average owner anyway. This is also a great opportunity to see how they do it if you're interested in trimming your dog's nails yourself later on.

Brushing Your Dog's Teeth

Unlike many of the other aspects of grooming, brushing your Tibetan Mastiff's teeth must be done every day in order to have any real affect on his dental health. Consider how healthy your own teeth would be if you only brushed them once per week or month. Excess tartar can build up quickly and result in serious health conditions, so it's important to keep a close eye on the condition of your dog's teeth. Dogs with periodontal disease experience pain, may be unable to eat, and may even lose teeth if left untreated. Additionally, bacteria from the plaque and tartar can enter your dog's bloodstream, potentially infecting vital organs. Thankfully, dental disease is completely preventable with a little at-home care combined with regular veterinary check-ups.

Your local pet store or favorite online retailer likely has a variety of toothbrushes and toothpastes to maintain your Tibetan Mastiff's dental health. Doggie toothbrushes often look the same as those made for human, but you can also find brushes that fit over the tip of your fingers. Use whatever works for you and your dog. For example, if you don't trust your dog not to bite down on a toothbrush, don't use the ones that fit over your finger. Toothpastes are also available in different flavors, ranging from chicken to vanilla. It's crucial that you use a toothpaste designed for dogs, rather than just using one made for humans. Human toothpaste often contains ingredients that be harmful to dogs. You can also make a paste out of baking soda and water if you'd prefer to make your own.

Even with daily at-home brushing, your Tibetan Mastiff is still going to need regular professional dental cleanings. Most veterinarians recommend cleanings every six to twelve months, depending on your dog's age and dental health. For this procedure, your dog will undergo anesthesia, but it is an incredibly safe procedure. If you have any questions or concerns about your dog's dental health or the cleaning procedure, don't be afraid to ask your veterinarian.

When Professional Help Is Necessary

"For the novice, find a groomer that is experienced with grooming double coats and take your TM in regularly. During the winter, weekly brushing should suffice. The big blow-out lasts for 30-40 days. A great groomer and regular schedule will minimize the impact of this if maintained regularly. NEVER shave a Tibetan Mastiff."

Debbie Parsons Slayton
Dreamcatcher Tibetan Mastiffs

Professional groomers are always available should you begin to struggle with any part of the grooming process. They are experts in handling difficult dogs, so don't be afraid to ask for help if you need it. Additionally, many groomers know how to gain a dog's trust, so even the most difficult dogs learn to stand patiently after just a few sessions. Dogs and owners may be nervous about their first grooming session, but finding a groomer you like and trust will make all the difference. Once your Tibetan Mastiff develops a relationship with his groomer, he may get excited whenever he has the opportunity to visit his new friend. Visiting the groomer is also an excellent opportunity for socialization.

You don't always need to be in a difficult situation to ask for professional grooming help. Many owners simply lack the time or willingness to groom their dogs themselves. This does not make you a bad owner. In fact, it's better to have a professional take care of the difficult task of grooming than put it off until you have time or are ready to do it yourself. There's absolutely no shame in seeking the service or advice of a professional groomer, so feel free to call on your local groomer to keep your Tibetan Mastiff looking and feeling his best

CHAPTER 16
Basic Health Care

"I would also recommend NOT spaying or neutering TMs (at least until you have a serious behavioral problem with one, then see a TM expert, not your vet, before doing it). No TM should be spayed or neutered before 18 months of age and you need to understand that it will create grooming hell for you if you do it. If you have multiple TM females that are not spayed you will have to separate them during their protracted heat cycles, from each other and from the male. TM females undergo a long pre-estrous before actually coming in heat and during this time they will be short tempered with other females and this is when most female/female fights happen."

Dr. Charles Radcliffe
Timberline Tibetan Mastiffs

Visiting the Vet

Scheduling routine veterinary appointments for your Tibetan Mastiff is essential in maintaining his health. Most vets recommend a basic examination every six to twelve months, depending on your dog's age and current health. It may seem silly to take your dog to the vet this often when he appears healthy, but it's important to be able to catch underlying conditions early and treat them as soon as possible. Many serious conditions can progress quickly if left untreated, so it's important to detect them early. Your Tibetan Mastiff will also need to be seen regularly in order to keep him on a proper schedule of vaccinations and deworming. Additionally, frequent visits give you and your vet the opportunity to discuss your dog's weight, overall health, and any potential health concerns.

Allergies

Allergy symptoms are caused by a hypersensitivity of your dog's immune system to a specific substance. The most common allergens are proteins from food, other animals, insects, or plants. Allergies are common in dogs of all breeds, with most being diagnosed as adults. Although some dogs may be diagnosed as young as six months of age, most symptoms don't show up until after one or two years of age.

Symptoms of allergies include localized or generalized itching, coughing, sneezing, and discharge from the eyes or nose. Some dogs, especially those with food allergies, may also experience vomiting and diarrhea. The way in which the allergen enters the body will likely be reflected in the symptoms. For instance, food allergies often appear as digestive upset,

while insect bite allergies will show up as localized itching or inflammation. Inhalant allergies, on the other hand, will cause the dog to experience respiratory problems and generalized itching.

Treatment for allergies will depend on the specific cause. For instance, if your Tibetan Mastiff is sensitive to certain proteins in his food, you'll need to monitor his diet closely. However, if your dog has environmental allergies, you may need use a combination of anti-inflammatory and antihistamine medication, either oral or injectable, with therapeutic shampoos or ointments. If you suspect your dog has allergies of any kind, be sure to discuss it with your vet as soon as possible. Without treatment, dogs with allergies can develop severe skin irritation including hot spots and hair loss. Respiratory symptoms should also be taken seriously and treated as soon as possible.

Fleas and Ticks

External parasites are a common source of dangerous diseases that can not only affect your Tibetan Mastiff, but your human family members as well. Fleas and ticks do not discriminate and can bite and transmit a variety of diseases to both humans and animals. Fleas are common carriers of both tapeworms and bartonellosis. Anemia is also common with heavy flea infestations. Flea allergy dermatitis is also possible, which is when your dog's immune system reacts negatively to the fleas' saliva. Symptoms of flea allergy dermatitis include inflammation of the skin, severe itching, and hair loss. Ticks are carriers of Lyme disease, ehrlichiosis, Rocky Mountain spotted fever, and babesiosis. The exact diseases carried by ticks vary according to location and climate. To keep your entire family safe from disease, administering

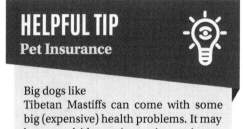

HELPFUL TIP
Pet Insurance

Big dogs like Tibetan Mastiffs can come with some big (expensive) health problems. It may be a good idea to invest in pet insurance while your Tibetan is young. All pet insurance plans have a waiting period before the coverage becomes active, and no pet insurance plans cover preexisting conditions. That's why it's important to sign up for a plan as soon as you bring your Tibetan Mastiff home.

flea and tick prevention medication must be a part of your dog's healthcare routine.

Depending on the area in which you live, you may or may not need to administer year-round flea and tick prevention. Warmer climates are more likely to have flea and tick problems all year than those with especially cold winters, where you may only need to treat your Tibetan Mastiff during the summer. Your veterinarian will be able to advise you on the proper schedule for treatment in your area. If you plan on boarding your dog or taking him to doggie daycare, you should also be aware that some facilities may require your dog to have received a recent dose of flea and tick prevention before he will be allowed to stay.

Ask your veterinarian which flea and tick prevention product is right for your Tibetan Mastiff. Different products are more effective against different species, so the answer will vary according to where you live. Most flea and tick products are packaged in a plastic vial, which can be broken at the end and applied to the back of your dog's neck. Since Tibetan Mastiffs often have a heavy coat around the neck, you'll need to part the hair in order to apply the product directly to the skin. Typically, this process is repeated every four to six weeks or so.

Flea and tick collars are also an option, but most experts strongly discourage the use of these products, especially if you have other pets in the home. Some brands of flea collar use insecticides such as tetrachlorvinphos, which can cause serious reactions. Cats are especially sensitive to this chemical. Reactions may vary from skin irritation and hair loss to gastrointestinal upset and even seizures. In some cases, especially with prolonged exposure, it can result in death. Tetrachlorvinphos is also considered a carcinogen by the Environmental Protection Agency, so you may also be putting your human family members at risk by using this product.

Internal Parasites

In addition to preventing fleas and ticks, you'll also want to make sure you deworm your Tibetan Mastiff regularly to prevent infection by internal parasites. Most internal parasites can cause serious health problems if left untreated, so regular deworming is crucial. The types of parasites that your dog may pick up will depend on the area you live in, but your local veterinarian will know what species are common in your region. Many internal parasites can be passed on to humans, and children can be especially susceptible to parasite infection, so keeping your dog parasite-free is essential in keeping your entire family healthy.

Intestinal worms are the most common internal parasites found in dogs. Puppies especially are prone to parasitic infections, which they typically pick up from adult dogs in the home. Worms are passed from host to host when one animal consume eggs or larvae found in contaminated water, food, soil, or feces. The most common types of intestinal worms in dogs are roundworms, hookworms, whipworms, and tapeworms. Worms aren't the only type of intestinal parasite, however, as your Tibetan Mastiff could become infected with protozoa such as giardia and coccidia. All of the parasites mentioned thus far infect the dog's intestines and digestive tract, but heartworms are another type of internal parasite that infect the heart and bloodstream. Heartworm is passed from host to host by mosquitos as they feed on the blood of various animals. Heartworm is far more complicated to treat than most of the other internal parasites and can be deadly. Treatment takes several months to complete, and the dog's activity and movement must be limited to prevent the dying worms from blocking arteries. Thankfully, heartworm is as easy to prevent as intestinal parasites, with a chewable tablet each month.

If your Tibetan Mastiff has become infected by internal parasites, you may notice symptoms such as vomiting, diarrhea, and weight loss. Dogs with an especially heavy load of parasites may have a distended stomach with an otherwise malnourished appearing body. Lethargy, anemia, and coughing are also common. Some dogs may not exhibit any symptoms at all, so regular testing and deworming are crucial.

Your local veterinarian will be able to detect intestinal worms and protozoa through a fecal exam. A small sample of your dog's feces will be collected and examined under a microscope. A veterinary professional will then search the sample for eggs or larvae. Ascertaining the type of parasite infecting your Tibetan Mastiff is essential in determining the correct course of treatment. Heartworm can only be detected through a blood test. After a small sample of blood has been taken, it is mixed with a chemical solution and place into a simple disposable testing device. After about fifteen minutes or so, the results will be ready to read. Treatment for most parasites will consist of either injections or oral medication. Depending on the specific type of infection, treatment may take anywhere from a couple of days to several months. Frequent testing and preventative deworming is key in preventing parasitic infections.

Vaccinations

All dogs will require vaccinations at some point in their lives. Core vaccines are those that are recommended no matter where you live, such as rabies, parvovirus, and distemper. Non-core vaccines, such as leptospirosis and Bordetella, may also be recommended depending on where you live and what kind of lifestyle your dog leads.

Typically, core vaccines are given in combination with a single syringe containing the antibodies for several different diseases. Sometimes referred to as a five-way, or DHPP, the most common vaccine protects against parvovirus, distemper, parainfluenza, hepatitis, and adenovirus cough. DHPP vaccines are initially given in a series of three at six, twelve, and sixteen weeks of age. Thereafter, they are given either yearly or every three years depending on your vet's recommendation.

The only vaccine that is required by law in the United States is the rabies vaccine. Rabies vaccines cannot be given before 16 weeks of age. The first vaccination is usually only good for a year, but later vaccinations may be effective for up to three years. Your vet will be able to recommend the correct schedule of vaccinations according to the laws in your area.

Your veterinarian may also recommend non-core vaccines such as leptospirosis, Lyme disease, and rattlesnake venom. If you board your Tibetan Mastiff frequently or take him to the groomer, you may also need the Bordetella vaccine, which prevents kennel cough. Non-core vaccines will vary according to your area and your dog's lifestyle, so ask for veterinarian for recommendations.

Although the majority of dogs are given vaccines without a problem, allergic reactions are possible. If you believe your Tibetan Mastiff to be sensitive to vaccines, you may want to talk to your vet about administering only one vaccine at a time so that you don't overwhelm your dog's system. Signs of an allergic reaction include hives, vomiting, lethargy, and swelling of the face or paws. Your dog may also experience swelling or pain around the injection site. Severe reactions can also include difficulty breathing and seizures. If your dog has not been vaccinated before, you may want to stay near the vet clinic for about twenty minutes so that you can be near help should he develop a reaction. Vaccine reactions can be life-threatening without proper treatment.

In some areas, titer testing is a legal alternative to yearly vaccines. A simple blood test is performed to measure the antibodies in your Tibetan Mastiff's blood. If the levels are high enough, the dog doesn't need to be vaccinated just yet, but if the levels are low, then he will require a vaccination to boost his immunity. Titer testing is typically only available for core vaccines as non-core vaccines do not last long enough to justify the effort and expense of titer testing. In some cases, titer testing may be more expensive than yearly vaccines, but if your dog is prone to vaccine reactions, it may be a better option to test rather than risk his health.

Holistic Alternatives

If you choose to live a more natural lifestyle and want the same for your Tibetan Mastiff, you may want to consider finding a holistic veterinarian in your city. Holistic veterinary medicine isn't just herbs and acupuncture, but instead is an appropriate combination of both conventional and alternative therapies. Holistic veterinarians went to the same schools as traditional veterinarians and will treat your pets with the same medications and procedures found in veterinary clinics across the country. However, those conventional therapies may also be combined with alternative treatments such as chiropractic adjustments, nutritional therapy, and acupuncture.

For pets with chronic conditions or conditions that have been difficult to treat with conventional veterinary medicine, holistic care can be especially beneficial. Holistic medicine treats the body as a whole, rather than a combination of individual parts. For example, if your Tibetan Mastiff suffers from arthritis in his hips, a holistic veterinarian may try to ease his pain using a combination of nutritional supplements, massage, and acupuncture. Instead of focusing solely on your dog's hip pain, a holistic vet will instead seek to improve your dog's overall health and wellbeing in an effort to improve the specific problem. This is not to say that alternative treatments should always be preferred over traditional medicine, especially in an emergency, but many owners find comfort in seeking a different solution to their pet's health condition.

If you're interested in finding a local holistic veterinarian, the American Holistic Veterinary Medical Association's website has a list of vets across the United States and Canada. The website allows you to search the vets by the species they treat as well as specific treatments that they may offer. This allows owners to find the perfect vet for their pet's particular needs.

Pet Insurance

Although veterinary care is not quite as expensive as human healthcare, the cost can be quite high for serious emergencies or illnesses. As costs rise, pet insurance is rising in popularity to help owners cover the cost of caring for their beloved animals. Different insurance companies offer different plans at a variety of price points and coverage amounts. You will be able to find a plan according to your budget or desired level of coverage. However, just as with human health insurance, some pets may require a higher monthly premium or may even be denied coverage due to certain

preexisting conditions. These limitations will vary by company so be sure to inquire if your Tibetan Mastiff has any current health issues.

It's important to note that unlike your own insurance, pet insurance does not typically cover the cost of routine or preventative care. Your Tibetan Mastiff's yearly exams and vaccinations will need to be paid for out of pocket. There are a few companies out there that offer coverage for preventative procedures, but plans are typically quite expensive. However, should your dog get into a serious accident or get diagnosed with cancer, pet insurance can be helpful in covering the high cost of treatment.

There are some owners who swear by pet insurance and would never go without it, while others would rather save their money for those possible emergencies. Owners who have experienced how helpful insurance can be are usually avid supporters, but owners with relatively healthy dogs may go years without filing a claim. Those years of monthly premiums for unused insurance policies can add up quickly, so some owners choose instead to put a sum of money aside each month into an emergency savings account for use in the event that their dog becomes injured or ill. Before you commit to buying pet insurance, do your research with several different insurance companies to make sure that it's right for you or if it's better to save your money.

CHAPTER 17
Health Concerns in Tibetan Mastiffs

"They have very few major problems so far as they are still a very primitive breed. The few issues are related to being a large breed such as bloat, epilepsy, hip and elbow dysplasia, and occasionally entropion or ectropion in the eyes. But compared to many breeds these conditions show up infrequently."

Michael Brantley
Dreamland Kennel

Genetic Testing

Tibetan Mastiffs are an incredibly healthy breed with few genetic problems. The frequency by which genetic disorders appear will depend on your dog's bloodlines. Reputable breeders will work hard to eliminate genetic problems by breeding only healthy dogs, but less reputable breeders may be willing to overlook genetic disorders in favor of factors such as size or coat that may sell for a higher price.

There are really only two genetic disorders common in the Tibetan Mastiff. One is Progressive Retinal Atrophy (PRA), which is a disease that affects the light sensitive photoreceptor cells at the back of the eye. The end result is a total loss of sight. The other is commonly referred to as Canine Inherited Demyelinative Neuropathy (CIDN) or Hypertrophic Neuropathy, though this condition is rarely found in the breed today. CIDN is a result of the degeneration of the protective covering of the nerve fibers, or myelin sheath. Once the myelin sheath has been damaged, nerve impulses are altered

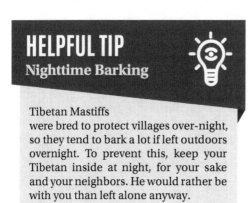

HELPFUL TIP
Nighttime Barking

Tibetan Mastiffs were bred to protect villages over-night, so they tend to bark a lot if left outdoors overnight. To prevent this, keep your Tibetan inside at night, for your sake and your neighbors. He would rather be with you than left alone anyway.

or stopped, which result in weakness, decreased reflexes, and an inability to bark. Both diseases can be debilitating, which is why it's important for breeders to perform genetic testing on their dogs prior to breeding.

Genetic testing in dogs is as simple as it is with human. DNA samples are painlessly collected through a sample of the individual dog's saliva. The sample is then submitted to an approved laboratory for genetic analysis. Once the sample has been analyzed, the results are made available so that the breeder can make an informed decision about whether an individual dog should be bred or if spaying or neutering is a better option. Using this responsible breeding practice, incidents of both PRA and CIDN within the Tibetan Mastiff breed are incredibly low.

Photo taken by Lei Song, Owners Jordan and Amanda Seevers

Kesang Camp's Sol-Lay Of Drakyi

Hip and Elbow Dysplasia

Hip dysplasia is a painful condition that is common in large breed dogs such as the Tibetan Mastiff. The disease, which can have either genetic or environmental causes, occurs when the ball and socket of the hip joint do not develop properly. The result is a join that rubs or grinds instead of sliding smoothly. The grinding will result in further deterioration and an eventual loss of function of the hip joint. Symptoms of hip dysplasia include decreased activity or range of motion of the hip, lameness, stiffness, or a reluctance to jump or run. Affected dogs might also experience a loss of muscle mass in the thigh as well as a unique hopping gait. Hip dysplasia is typically diagnosed through a combination of physical examination and x-rays. Treatments available will depend on the severity of the condition, but may range from changes in nutrition and exercise to surgery and medication.

Elbow dysplasia is similar to hip dysplasia in that it's due to a malformation of the joint. However, elbow dysplasia actually encompasses several conditions such as fragmented coronoid process (FCP), osteochondrosis (OCD), and cartilage anomaly. The specific conditions simply refer to the exact malformation within the joint. As with hip dysplasia, it's most common in large breed dogs. This is a painful condition that typically worsens

Photo Courtesy of Richard Eichhorn & Efrain Valle Drakyi Tibetan Mastiffs

GCH Drakyi Legend of Olympus, ZEUS & Drakyi Leonidas, LEO

over time, especially without treatment. Symptoms include front end lameness and in severe cases an unwillingness to stand up or walk. Elbow dysplasia can affect one or both elbow joints. Lameness can sometimes be difficult to detect when both joints are affected as the gait will not appear asymmetrical.

Although not every case of hip and elbow dysplasia can be prevented, reputable breeders will do their best to make sure that their breeding stock are free from these debilitating conditions. The Orthopedic Foundation for Animals (OFA) allows breeders to submit x-rays for assessment before making the results publicly available on their website. In order for results to be posted, breeders must submit a series of required and optional test results and information. For the Tibetan Mastiff, both hip and elbow x-rays must be submitted for evaluation.

Eye Problems

As previously mentioned, Progressive Retinal Atrophy (PRA) is a genetic eye disease that affects the photoreceptors of the eye. There are two different types of PRA. The first is sometimes referred to as retinal dysplasia and is typically diagnosed in puppies at around two to three months of age. The other type is a late onset form that is usually diagnosed between three and nine years of age. In the early onset form, the photoreceptor cells simply develop abnormally, leading to blindness at an early age. However, with the late onset form, the photoreceptor cells of the retina may develop normally, but they degenerate over time. One of the early signs of PRA is night blindness, so affected dogs may be reluctant to move around in the dark or may bump into things.

It should be noted that although PRA is not a painful condition, it is a progressive disease and the vision of dogs with PRA will slowly deteriorate until the dog is completely blind. The timeframe from onset to complete loss of vision typically takes a year or two. Unfortunately, there is no treatment for PRA. Some veterinarians may recommend antioxidant supplements, but there is no proof that these supplements slow the progression of the disease. Fortunately, most dogs can function well without eyesight. Dogs tend to rely more on their other senses and will quickly develop a mental map of their home so that they can move about without trouble. However, dogs affected with PRA should not be bred as they can pass the condition to their offspring.

Another hereditary abnormality of the eye that can be found in Tibetan Mastiffs is entropion. Entropion is a condition in which the dog's eyelid rolls inward, causing the eyelashes to rub against the cornea. This is a painful condition and affected dogs may squint, keep their eye shut, and produce excess tears. Usually, both eyes are affected, and dogs are diagnosed prior to their first birthday.

The only treatment for entropion is surgical correction. A sliver of skin is removed from the outer surface of the eyelid and stitched together to roll

Photo Courtesy of Maria Folkomina

the eyelid outward. The correction is often performed as a series of two sur-
geries, with a major correction first and a minor correction later. This is to
prevent an over-correction of the condition, causing the eyelid to roll outward. Even if dogs are diagnosed at a young age, most will not undergo surgical intervention until they reach maturity. In the meantime, affected dogs
may be treated with ophthalmic medications to lubricate the eye and protect the cornea.

Autoimmune Disorders

Autoimmune thyroiditis is a common condition in Tibetan Mastiffs and
is the most common cause of hypothyroidism in dogs of all breeds. Hypothyroidism is when the thyroid gland does not produce enough of a hormone called thyroxine. Thyroxine is responsible for controlling the metabolism, so dogs with hypothyroidism tend to be overweight and may also
suffer from skin issues and hair loss. Most dogs with autoimmune thyroiditis are diagnosed between two and five years of age, but dogs of any age
can be affected. The disease can be detected prior to the appearance of
clinical signs through a blood test. The presence of thyroglobulin autoanti-
body formation in the blood signals the onset of the disease.

Hypothyroidism is not a life-threatening or painful disease. In fact, it's
easy and inexpensive to diagnose, treat, and maintain. Treatment typically consists of a low-cost daily oral tablet. Although this disease is not serious, Tibetan Mastiffs diagnosed with autoimmune thyroiditis should not
be bred. This is why the OFA recommends that dogs be tested periodically
throughout their lives. In order to receive their OFA number, so that results
can be made publicly available, dogs must be tested and found normal at
one year of age. Of course, dogs can be tested at any age, but if done before twelve months of age, the results will not be submitted to the OFA database. The OFA recommends retesting at two, three, four, six, and eight
years of age.

Ear Infections

Otitis externa, also known as an outer ear infection, is a common condition in dogs with floppy or hairy ears. Since Tibetan Mastiffs have both floppy ears and a thick, wooly mane, ear infections can be a problem with the
breed. Ear infection can be quite painful, and you may notice your dog shak-
ing his head or vigorously scratching his ear. The ears usually have an un-

pleasant odor and may be red or inflamed. In more severe cases, the ears may also appear thick or crusty.

Thankfully, ear infections are easy to diagnose and treat. Your vet will take a sample of the discharge from the affected ear to determine whether it is due to the overgrowth of yeast or bacteria. Once the cause is determined, the right medication can be prescribed. Typically, infections are treated with liquid medication that must be applied directly into the ear canal, but severe infections may also be supplemented with oral medication.

To prevent your Tibetan Mastiff from developing ear infections, it's important to keep his ears as clean and dry as possible. After swimming and baths, be sure to clean his ears to remove excess moisture. This moisture, in combination with your dog's body temperature, creates the perfect environment for yeast and bacteria to thrive. Even if your dog doesn't get wet often, it's crucial to regularly check his ears and clean them as needed. Monitoring the health of your Tibetan Mastiff's ears will allow you to catch any problems in their early stages and seek treatment as soon as possible. Ear infections can be quite painful so it's best to deal with the problem sooner rather than later.

Preventing Illnesses

Although not every disease can be prevented, properly managing your Tibetan Mastiff's lifestyle, nutrition, and healthcare can make a difference in preventing serious health problems. As your dog's caretaker, it's your responsibility to provide him with the best care possible. This means feeding him a high-quality diet, exercising, and grooming him regularly, in addition to regular veterinary care.

One of the most important aspect of keeping your Tibetan Mastiff healthy and free from disease is making regular appointments with your local veterinarian. It can seem frivolous to take your dog to the vet every six months or so if he seems healthy, but frequent examinations are essential in catching problems early. Many conditions can progress quickly, so it's important to catch them in their early stages if possible. Regular visits also give you the opportunity to bring up your dog's weight, overall condition, and any concerns that you may have. Additionally, regular visits will ensure that your dog stays up to date on his vaccinations and deworming schedule.

CHAPTER 18
The Aging Tibetan Mastiff

Basics of Senior Dog Care

Large breeds, such as Tibetan Mastiffs, are generally considered to be senior, or geriatric, at around six or seven years of age. Of course, this doesn't mean that your dog's lifestyle should change as soon as he celebrates his sixth birthday. Depending on your dog's health, he may begin to slow down earlier, or he may display the vitality of his youth well into his senior years. With a life expectancy of ten to twelve years on average, Tibetan Mastiffs tend to start slowing down after about six or seven years of age.

As your Tibetan Mastiff ages, you may begin noticing subtle changes in his body and behavior. Perhaps he's sleeping more or getting tired more quickly on his daily walks. Some older dogs can be quite stiff in the morning and may have difficulty getting out of bed. Deteriorating sight and hearing are also common with aging Tibetan Mastiffs, so be sure to use extra caution around your dog if he seems like he can't see or hear as well as he used to. You don't want to surprise him if you wake him from a nap or suddenly appear next to him. Some older dogs will gain weight as their metabolism slows, but others may become quite thin. Bathroom breaks will also need to be more frequent as many seniors can't hold it as long as they used to. Some geriatric dogs may also develop symptoms of cognitive dysfunction, or dementia, and may behave differently or seem confused at times. Richard Eichhorn of Drakyi Tibetan Mastiffs also recommends yearly thyroid screening for senior Tibetan Mastiffs. As you notice these changes, it's crucial that you adjust your dog's care to accommodate him in this stage of his life.

HELPFUL TIP
Can Your Older Tibetan Get Around Your Home?

Like many other large-dog breeds, Tibetan Mastiffs are more prone to bone and joint prob¬lems with age. That can make it harder for them to get around as they get older. Does your home have a lot of steps? Does it have slippery flooring? Keep in mind that you may need to carry your 150-pound dog up or down those stairs when he gets older if you don't have ramps where appropriate.

Photo Courtesy
of Anne-Teresa Luciani

Multi CH Drakyi Indira Of Haleigha

Regular Vet Visits

Most vets will recommend more frequent visits as your dog ages. If you were taking your Tibetan Mastiff in for examinations every year, you may want to consider taking him every four to six months or so instead. Not only will this give your vet the chance to catch any developing conditions in their early stages, but it will give you a chance to discuss any concerns you might have as well. If your dog's behavior seems to be changing, or you notice significant changes in weight, you want to address these problems as soon as possible. Additionally, older dogs may require more frequent dental care than they did in their youth.

With each vet visit, be sure to ask your vet for recommendations to help make your dog's transition into old age easier. The vet may suggest changes in nutrition or exercise, or just ways to make your beloved companion more comfortable as he ages. She may also recommend that you bring your Tibetan Mastiff in more frequently to monitor any diseases or conditions as they develop.

Nutritional Changes

One of the most common nutritional changes experienced by aging Tibetan Mastiffs is the number of calories they require. As dogs age, their metabolisms tend to slow, which can lead to weight gain if their diet is not adjusted accordingly. Excess weight can be especially damaging to aging, arthritic joints. As dogs gain weight, they may experience more joint pain, leading to less mobility and more weight gain. To prevent the health challenges associated with obesity, it's important to adjust your Tibetan Mastiff's daily meals to accommodate his changing body. This may mean smaller portion sizes, or you might consider switching him to food formulated for senior dogs. Senior dog foods tend to contain fewer calories but may also contain other beneficial ingredients such as glucosamine, chondroitin, and increased fiber.

Not all aging Tibetan Mastiffs will gain weight as their metabolism changes. Some older dogs may find it difficult to keep weight on and may become quite thin. These dogs often have changes in appetite and will turn their nose up at foods they once found irresistible. For these types of seniors, you may need to change your food to accommodate your dog's changing

*Photo Courtesy
of Maria Folkomina*

interest in food. You'll need to find a way to make his food more appetizing, which might mean changing his diet entirely or simply adding tasty toppers to his daily meals. For kibble-fed dogs, you might consider switching to or simply adding canned food. Some owners also choose to supplement their senior dog's meals with raw or cooked food. It may take some experimentation to find what interests your aging dog, but it's crucial that you ensure that he gets enough food to maintain a healthy weight.

Depending on your senior dog's overall health, you may also need to adjust his diet according to any health conditions that he's developed. Tibetan Mastiffs with heart or kidney problems may need to be fed a prescription diet, rather than a senior dog formula. The pain of arthritis is often dealt with by adding joint supplements to senior dog's diets. Ingredients such as MSM, glucosamine, and chondroitin can help make your dog more comfortable in his golden years. Some dogs may also experience digestive issues which may require supplements such as fiber, probiotics, or digestive enzymes. Before adding any supplements to your dog's diet, or if you notice sudden changes in your dog's weight, be sure to have a discussion with your veterinarian. It's important to rule out any health problems before changing or adding to your Tibetan Mastiff's diet.

Exercising Your Senior Dog

Aching, arthritic joints and a slowing metabolism can make even the most energetic Tibetan Mastiff slow down as he ages. Certain health problems may also exacerbate your dog's discomfort with strenuous exercise. As your dog begins to experience more discomfort during exercise, it can be tempting to let him lie around on the sofa all day instead of going for his daily walks. However, eliminating exercise from your senior dog's daily schedule isn't recommended. Exercise is essential to every senior dog's health, but you will need to adjust his physical activity levels to accommodate his changing body. You may need to provide him with shorter, more frequent exercise sessions instead of a daily hours-long walk.

You may also want to consider exchanging sessions of vigorous physical activity for more mental work. Mental exercise is a great way to keep your senior Tibetan Mastiff active and busy without putting unnecessary strain on his body. Many older dogs experience a slowing down of their bodies long before their minds, so they may find joy in activities requiring them to use more of their mind. Activities such as puzzle toys or scent work can be a great way to keep your dog stimulated and engaged without causing physical discomfort.

As your Tibetan Mastiff ages, you may also need to adjust the environment in which he exercises. Slick floors, long flights of stairs, and hard pavement can spell trouble for senior dogs. Rather than an indoor game of fetch or a long walk on concrete, consider letting your senior dog wander through grass or on a dirt trail. The change in scenery is a great way to add a little mental stimulation to your daily walks and the softer surface will provide a bit more comfort to your dog's weakening muscles and aching joints.

Environmental Changes

In addition to changing the environment where you exercise your Tibetan Mastiff, you may also need to alter his home environment to accommodate age-related changes. Senior dogs do not have the strength they once had in their muscles, so they may not be able to handle hard flooring like tile or hardwood. You might consider placing more rugs around your house or having your dog wear non-slip booties to prevent him from falling. Dementia can cause older dogs to become confused, so you'll need to protect your dog from accidentally finding himself in a stairwell, in the pool, or outside of the yard. The changes experienced in old age may require you to limit your Tibetan Mastiff's access to your home or property, but it may be necessary to do so for his health and safety. If you notice your dog struggling to get up onto the furniture, you'll need to provide him with lower alternative beds or stairs to ease his way up onto the sofa or bed. While these changes may not be the best choices for your décor, your aging dog's wellbeing should always be your priority.

Common Old Age Ailments

Arthritis is one of the most common ailments experienced by aging Tibetan Mastiffs. You may notice a stiffness or slowness in your dog, especially in the mornings or after a nap. Be sure to accommodate these changes with joint care supplements, cushier or elevated beds, and less strenuous exercise. You might also notice that your Tibetan Mastiff becomes easily confused or startled. Even if he's not developing dementia, a loss in hearing or sight can make a once confident dog much more cautious, especially in the dark. You'll need to be more careful to announce your presence to your aging dog and be careful not to startle him from naps. Some senior dogs can be somewhat difficult to manage in their later years, but even during these tough times it's important to remember the many years of joy you've shared with your beloved Tibetan Mastiff.

Preparing to Say Goodbye

As your Tibetan Mastiff ages or his health declines, you'll need to begin planning for the end of your beloved companion's life. In cases of extreme illness, it may be obvious when it's time to call your vet, but with aging, it can be difficult to know when it's the right time to say goodbye. Quality of life should be the main factor in determining whether euthanasia is the right option. If your dog no longer seems as happy as he once did or his moments of suffering outnumber his moments of joy, you may need to make a serious decision. As you approach the end of your time together, it's important to reflect on your beloved Tibetan Mastiff's life and all of the happiness he has given you over the years. Saying goodbye is never easy, but remembering the good times can help you navigate through your grief.

Some dogs may die peacefully in their sleep as the effects of old age overcome them. For others, they may need assistance in the form of humane euthanasia. Euthanasia is a painless procedure where a veterinarian administers an overdose of an anesthesia drug called sodium pentobarbital. When injected into the bloodstream, sodium pentobarbital causes the recipient to fall asleep before gently stopping the heart. The procedure is typically performed while the dog is lying down, either on a table or on the floor of your home or an exam room. A veterinary technician may help hold the dog so that the drug can be injected by the veterinarian, usually into a vein in the front leg via an intravenous catheter. If the dog is unused to being handled by strangers or is confused or afraid, a sedative may be given first to put the dog at ease. One the sodium pentobarbital has been inject-

ed, unconsciousness usually occurs in a matter of seconds and the heart will stop within a minute or two. The veterinarian will then use a stethoscope to confirm that the heart has stopped.

As the end nears, you may want to consider discussing your options for your Tibetan Mastiff's final arrangements. This can be a difficult thing to talk about in the moment, but arranging everything with your vet in advance can help ease the stress during your last moments together. Many vets offer both in-office and in-home euthanasia services. For some dogs and owners, it can be stressful to say goodbye in the unfamiliar environment of an exam room. For others, they may not want the memories of these final moments in their home. Whichever you prefer, your veterinary team is sure to be comforting and supportive during this difficult time. The most important aspect of saying goodbye is being with your Tibetan Mastiff. In his last moments, he will be comforted knowing that he's beside the person or people he loves the most.

After you've said goodbye, your veterinarian will likely have several options available for your Tibetan Mastiff's remains. If you would prefer not to deal with them yourself, your veterinary team of choice will be happy to make arrangements for your beloved companion's remains. You may also be able to request cremation. With cremation, you may be able to have your dog's ashes returned to you. Some vets may return the ashes in a simple box, while others may offer a variety of urns. If you know the time is coming, it can be helpful to discuss your options prior to saying goodbye so that you can focus on your last moments with your Tibetan Mastiff, knowing that arrangements have already been made.

Grief and Healing

After saying goodbye to your Tibetan Mastiff, you may experience a difficult period of grief. The first few days and weeks will be especially hard, but it will get easier with time. Many owners choose to create a memorial for their dogs to help them remember their most treasured moments together. Personalized jewelry, garden stones, and tiles can be found to memorialize your beloved companion. Some owners also channel their grief into helping others by planting trees or flower gardens, or volunteering at a local animal shelter. Making a difference in the lives of others can be a beneficial part of many owners' grieving processes. If you are struggling to move on with the healing process, you may also consider seeking counseling or discussing your grief with a professional. Everyone processes grief differently, so find what brings comfort to you and your family. However you choose to heal, be sure to cherish your memories together and remember the unconditional love your Tibetan Mastiff gave you.

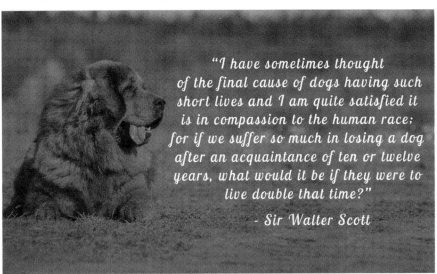

"I have sometimes thought of the final cause of dogs having such short lives and I am quite satisfied it is in compassion to the human race; for if we suffer so much in losing a dog after an acquaintance of ten or twelve years, what would it be if they were to live double that time?"

- Sir Walter Scott

Made in the USA
Las Vegas, NV
16 March 2024

87324388R00101